Age of Enlightenment

A Captivating Guide to the Age of Reason, Including the Lives of Isaac Newton, Francis Bacon, John Locke, and Mary Somerville

Free Bonus from Captivating History (Available for a Limited time)

Hi History Lovers!

Now you have a chance to join our exclusive history list so you can get your first history ebook for free as well as discounts and a potential to get more history books for free! Simply visit the link below to join.

Captivatinghistory.com/ebook

Also, make sure to follow us on Facebook, Twitter and Youtube by searching for Captivating History.

Contents

Introduction

The Age of Enlightenment—also known as the Age of Reason—was a philosophical and intellectual movement that mainly took place in Europe, and subsequently in North America, in the 17th and 18th centuries. People who believed in the spirit of the age believed that after the centuries spent in the so-called Dark Ages (also known as the Middle Ages) following the collapse of the ancient Roman Empire, enlightened human intellect and culture had come forward once more. In the French and American Revolutions and constitutions, the philosophy of this new age was highly influential and formative.

The Enlightenment was greatly influenced by the preceding Scientific Revolution and, before that, the Renaissance. Each era, beginning with the European Renaissance in the 14th century and then the Scientific Revolution in the 16th century, led Europeans to create a new culture in which higher education and the arts were valued more highly than any other endeavor. Regular education spread throughout the continent, beginning mostly in wealthy families but slowly spreading among the children of agricultural and lower-class families as well.

Starting in the 14th century, European aristocrats favored a classical education that hearkened back to the days of the ruling Roman

Empire. Believing that the Greeks and Romans were the epitomai of intellectual culture, many Europeans wanted to return to that age of intellectualism and artistry—and thus, the Renaissance was born. From Ireland to Russia, Greek- and Roman-style architecture flourished alongside engineering and mathematics lessons. A few centuries later, it was impossible to ignore the fact that science had become a primary trade. With the help of Galileo Galilei, Isaac Newton, and many other natural philosophers, the Scientific Revolution transformed the way an almost entirely religious land approached both existential and logical questions.

The life of an eminent scientist during the Scientific Revolution and the ensuing Enlightenment was not easy. Many learned, ambitious people were killed in the name of the Catholic Church for their scientific and philosophical works, which were often viewed as heretical. As time went on, however, and the truths of scientific research and exploration showed themselves time and time again, the collective perspective of the population began to shift away from religious dogma toward the logical scientific method.

The Enlightenment gained traction in the 17th century, and more emphasis was given to scientific techniques in the schools, as well as to the separation of religious and scientific data. Religious philosophies also became less rooted in the exact words of the Catholic Church, as papal authority gave way in many European countries to splinter groups of Christianity, such as the Calvinists, Lutherans, and other types of Protestants.

Major figures of the Enlightenment period include Voltaire, Isaac Newton, John Locke, Thomas Hobbes, David Hume, Jean-Jacques Rousseau, Adam Smith, Immanuel Kant, and Thomas Jefferson. These and many other great thinkers of the era influenced mass social upheaval in pursuit of equality and human rights, and many historians consider the culmination of these efforts to have been the French Revolution of 1789.

Chapter 1 – The Republic of Letters

(17th and 18th centuries)

Europe's ascent out of the Middle Ages was characterized by widespread education, the expansion of the sciences, and religious reforms. The patchwork of countries, duchies, and principalities that comprised the continent changed at top-speed during the 16th century as explorers discovered whole new worlds and scientists discovered the underpinnings of physical life as they knew it. Though information could only travel as swiftly as a horse or a mail ship, communication was integral to the spread of scientific revelations, geographical colonization, religious laws, and politics. To facilitate the dissemination of the most important news of the day, educated and philosophically-minded men established the Republic of Letters.

The term "men" in this case is not used lightly; the community consisted mainly of aristocratic men, owing to the social limitations of females and those of poor means. Female members of European society were rarely allowed the same education and career opportunities as their male counterparts, and therefore, the Republic of Letters was almost exclusively the domain of men. There were a few important exceptions, however, including Princess Elisabeth of Bohemia, Anna Maria van Schurman, Marie de Gournay, Lady Ranelagh, Marie du Moulin, Dorothy Moore, Bathsua Makin, and Katherine Jones.

In contrast, countless men took part in the Republic of Letters and the overall Enlightenment, though their numbers generally only included the sons of wealthy families. Participants ranged from René Descartes and Isaac Newton to Benjamin Franklin and Adam Smith. With easy access to political jobs, important diplomatic roles at the courts of their monarchs, and the full right to publicly speak and publish books in their own names, men were destined to shape the bulk of the Enlightenment, just as males had done in the Renaissance. Fortunately, the philosophical ideals of the Enlightenment would help free women and the poor from some of their social restraints.

The Republic of Letters was a long-distance network that connected intellectuals in Europe and America throughout the centuries of the Enlightenment. The network promoted communications between the scientists, theologians, and philosophers of the time so that each could stay up to date on subjects such as astronomy, chemistry, and Protestantism. In the 17th century, the Republic of Letters was nothing less than a self-proclaimed society of academics and literary figures that extended across domestic borders but respected the distinctions between language and culture.

The first documented occurrence of the term "Republic of Letters" in Latin takes place within a letter from Francesco Barbaro to Poggio Bracciolini. Barbaro was a successful Venetian politician who translated many important Greek manuscripts into Latin; Bracciolini was responsible for salvaging many of those original manuscripts from the forgotten corners of European monastic libraries. Barbaro's letter, dated July 6th, 1417, praised Bracciolini for "bringing to this Republic of Letters the largest number of aids and equipments."[1]

In Barbaro's and Bracciolini's day, it was still the early Renaissance, when classical education was coming back into fashion throughout Europe and, with it, a deep love and respect for knowledge. Thanks largely to the work of these two Italian scholars, Greek and Latin languages would flourish for another four centuries. Personal letters during this era were often written as if addressing an entire group of people instead of merely one recipient since correspondence that was deemed important was forwarded many times to reach several individuals. In this way, it was easy to maintain a line of communication that included dozens of recipients and writers. The letters were usually written in Latin or French in the first years of the network, but soon, there was a great demand for translations and original works in German and Dutch.

Within the 17th-century Republic of Letters, not only hand-written letters were exchanged, but documents, pamphlets, and fliers were as well. For the men of the Republic, it was considered to be one's duty to expand the community by recruiting like-minded individuals and passing along current documents. Several people created print journals to pass along the network, including the *Journal des Sçavans* and *Nouvelles de le république des lettres*. Journals, being shorter and lighter than books and also quicker to write and produce, revolutionized the spread of intellectual information and were passed along postal networks with individual commentary and notes.

Though the publication of journals satisfied the desire of information for most members of the Republic of Letters, they were still slower than individual letters. Therefore, journals did not replace the exchange of letters but merely added to it. An additional outcome of journal publication was an expanded readership and curiosity for scientific information among the countries of Europe, as well as

---

[1] Van Miert, Dirk. "What was the Republic of Letters?" University of Groningen Press.

North America. Contemporary ideas in medicine, physics, and other such topics had begun to be consumed by far more literate people than ever before, which fueled societal interest in science and had a huge influence on the Enlightenment as a whole.

In a way, the letter-writing networks of the Enlightenment opened up scientific, theological, and philosophical subjects to an audience that would otherwise have had little information on such topics. Science became a common interest and a hobby of many people who had not necessarily attended university or pursued a career in a related field. As an interesting side effect of the spread of scientific knowledge throughout Europe, the religious powers that be began to lose their tight grip on the continent.

Chapter 2 – Michel de Montaigne

(1533-1592)

Born in France, Michel de Montaigne was an intellectual and essayist who grew up disappointed by the decline of the European Renaissance. Whereas in the years before his birth France and other countries had been full of hope and plans for the sciences and literature of the day, that excitement had calmed significantly during Montaigne's lifetime. Believing that the world was still very much in need of new ideas and higher education, Montaigne dedicated himself to the production of essays in which he examined his own characteristics and humanity. These self-portraits, as many call them, were designed to help readers learn more about their own character and the ways in which they are similar to their fellow humans.

Montaigne, in his childhood, was taught at home. He had a classical education in which the only language of instruction was Latin; in fact, Montaigne did not receive lessons in his own vernacular until the age of six.

When Montaigne reached an appropriate age, his studies continued at the Collège de Guyenne. Unfortunately, he encountered a regime of strict discipline there that he found hostile and unproductive. He moved on to the University of Toulouse to study law and received a degree that allowed him to follow in his family's footsteps as a civil servant. In 1557, he became a member of the Parliament of Bordeaux, one of the eight regional parliaments that constituted the French Parliament.

It was after he established a career for himself within the French government that Montaigne began to explore his writing skills. Part of this was inspired by his friendship with the older humanist writer and civil servant Étienne de la Boétie, for whom Montaigne wrote one of his first essays, "On Friendship."

Montaigne wrote quite touchingly about his relationship with la Boétie, which was likely a kind of mentorship. According to the author, the relationship was not only ideal for the pair but better than all other human relationships Montaigne could think of. Theirs was clearly a productive and satisfying alliance, as not only could Montaigne and la Boétie exchange ideas about their work within the French Parliament, but they could also discuss and theorize about the state of the human condition in relation to religion and government policy.

La Boétie passed away in 1563, leaving behind his younger friend to grieve terribly.[2] Though the humanist and scholar left a hole in Montaigne's life that no other being could fill, historians believe that this event led to Montaigne's pursuance of full-time writing. Six years after the death of his dear friend, Montaigne put pen to paper to try to puzzle out the mysteries of life and loss on his own.

While Montaigne concentrated on his work, his father made a request: that he translate a book of natural philosophy written by Raymond Sebond, a Spanish monk. Sadly, the elder Montaigne died before the work could be published, but his son gave the work to the press in 1569. The result was *An Apology for Raymond Sebond*, a book in which Montaigne actually defends the position of the first

---

[2] Calhoun, Alison. *Montaigne and the Lives of the Philosophers*. 2014.

author in his belief that science cannot properly explain matters of religion.

The very next year, Montaigne retired from the Parliament of Bordeaux by selling his seat—a perfectly legal move at the time. Preparing to move into his father's château, which had been bequeathed to him in the will, he had Boétie's unpublished work sent to the printing press and moved back to the southwest of France, which was where Montaigne's family home was located. He resettled into the château and devoted himself to becoming a major force in French literature.

Montaigne set to work in a library packed with books written in Greek and Latin, the very books which had been used in his primary education. It was a tumultuous time in France, as Henry III had just inherited the crown of France from his brother, Charles IX, and he maintained a strained relationship with Henry IV, King of Navarre. Navarre was a small but politically powerful kingdom located between France and Spain, and under the rule of Henry IV, it was a largely Protestant nation. Henry III was a staunch Roman Catholic, and the two kings were at odds because the King of Navarre stood to inherit the throne of France due to his familial relationship with Henry III. To calm the political situation, Henry IV promised to convert to Catholicism upon the death of his counterpart.

As for the *Essays* of the Catholic Montaigne, they ostensibly earned the respect of both kings, though there were a great many religious and political extremists who criticized the man openly. Their criticisms were based on the many chapters of Montaigne's *Essays*, which were written between the years 1570 and 1592 and first published in 1580. Written in the French vernacular, despite the author's upbringing to respect only Latin and Greek work, the *Essays'* proclaimed purpose was to be very honest and transparent. Through his writings, which were extremely popular, Montaigne expressed insight into the human nature, which excited his readers.

Despite his many attempts to find clarity on the subject of life and nature, Montaigne never found a satisfying answer to his own inquiries and existential questions. He mistrusted the existing information he studied but could find no reasonable alternative within logic and science. He eventually concluded that while humans are finite and bound by their own physical constraints, the truth is infinite. Therefore, the human capacity to fully grasp the many truths of the universe is fatally flawed.

Facing unwanted critics within France, and altogether tired of the intellectual scene in his home country, Montaigne embarked upon a journey through several other European countries beginning in 1580. Over the course of fifteen months, the essayist visited other French cities, as well as locations in Germany, Austria, Switzerland, and Italy. Curious by nature, Montaigne was keenly interested in the smallest details of daily life within these foreign communities. Within these new environments, he searched for clues to his eternal search for the truth. His journey, written up as his *Journal de voyage*, included exciting depictions of picturesque scenes, meetings between new people, and fondly recorded reminiscences. The journal was personal and would not be published until after Montaigne's death.

Following his long journey, Montaigne was appointed mayor of Bordeaux, and at the insistence of King Henry III himself, he was convinced to return. He served as mayor for two terms before looking once more to writing. The political environment of France was becoming more strained during that period, and the author was arrested by members of the Protestant League in Paris, though he was soon allowed to return home. He fervently published multiple chapters of his *Essays* between his jobs serving as a diplomatic negotiator between the Catholic and Protestant kings.

The last years of Montaigne's life were characterized by ongoing diplomatic work, which was not always successful. After the assassination of Henry III in 1589, he helped smooth over the transfer of power to Henry IV, who, despite his earlier promise to become Catholic, clung to his Protestant upbringing.[3] The noted essayist died in 1592, having recently met one of his most ardent fans, Marie de Gournay. She would help to carry on his legacy and further explore the mysteries of existence that had been such a formative part of Montaigne's life.

---

[3] "Michel de Montaigne." *Encyclopedia Britannica*. Web.

Chapter 3 – Francis Bacon

(1561-1626)

Francis Bacon can be described as the quintessential Renaissance man and one of the first personalities of the Enlightenment. He worked in politics, science, philosophy, and even wrote plays during his career and was one of the last appointed legal counselors of Queen Elizabeth I of England. When the queen died in 1603, the new king, James I of England and Ireland (and known as James VI of Scotland), kept Bacon on, first making him a knight of the realm. Beginning in 1608, Bacon served the Crown officially. First serving as a clerk within the king's special judiciary Star Chamber, Bacon managed to stay on James' good side despite the king's feud over money with the Star Chamber and the group's later dissolution.

Despite holding a variety of positions within the court, Francis Bacon held a large number of debts that proved too much for even his good salary to fix. He used his reputation with the king to pursue a series of better positions under the Crown. His career soared, and in 1617, he was named lord high chancellor of England. However, his personal interests did not just include politics but also science. Three years after becoming the king's right-hand man, Bacon published *Novum Organum, sive indicia vera de Interpretatione Naturae,* or *New organon, or true directions concerning the interpretation of nature.* In *Novum,* he outlined a specific way to conduct scientific research that he believed should become common practice.

The Baconian Method, as it would come to be called, was reductionist in nature. He explained that the key to making a scientific discovery was deduction and careful research. For example, if one wanted to discover the source of a phenomenon such as light, one would create a list containing all the scenarios or objects known to contain light. Next, one would list all things that are never a source of light, even though they might be similar in other aspects to the things on the first list. On the third list, one should include items that contain light in varying circumstances. Finally, one might ascertain that the source of light is something common to everyone on the first list, absent in every item of the second, and sometimes active in items on the third.

The purpose of the proposed new scientific method of natural philosophy was to keep research and experimentation regimented, repeatable, and as thorough as possible. It was a divergence from the well-established Aristotelian Method, in which philosophers were encouraged to use a dialectic approach to their research. Dialectic, in the style of Aristotle's own writing, involved multiple points of view and discussion on a subject before making any claims. Its principles had held strong since the 4th century BCE, but with science taking over the world, more regimented methods such as that of Francis Bacon were better suited for the age.

Bacon had a very good reason to search for a cleaner, more succinct method of research, as did all natural philosophers: a desire for unbiased conclusions. According to Francis Bacon, human nature leads people to begin research with an idea already in mind as to what the results will be. Therefore, all study and experimentation are aimed at proving that claim whether or not the scientist realizes it. A clear scientific method could remove a great deal of biased information from the collective data, making the work of future scientists more trustworthy.

In tandem with his ideas for methodology, Bacon created the concept that all knowledge should be categorized neatly for easy reference. He realized that a wealth of information was only of use to the world if it could be accessed, edited, and added to as needed. Therefore, Bacon advised that known subjects be organized under the general headings of history, poetry, and philosophy. These categories aligned perfectly with the three features Bacon believed comprised human thought: memory, imagination, and reason.

In 1621, Bacon's career in government and politics came to an end when he was tried and found guilty of accepting bribes as a public servant. Historians feel that it is quite likely that he accepted gifts and money in exchange for services, as such behavior was commonplace at the court during that era. While under arrest, the disgraced lord chancellor wrote to his king to beg for forgiveness, protesting that he had only accepted gifts on the monarch's behalf and had intentions to pass it onto James I.

> MAY it please your most excellent Majesty,
>
> In the midst of my misery, which is rather assuaged by remembrance than by hope, my chiefest worldly comfort is to think, That...I was evermore so happy as to have my poor services graciously accepted by your Majesty...For as I have often said to your Majesty, I was towards you but as a bucket, and a cistern; to draw forth and conserve; whereas yourself was the fountain.[4]

The court fined him £40,000 and sent him to the Tower of London to serve a jail term, and though he managed to pay it and be released in

---

[4] Letter from Francis Bacon to King James I of England. Circa 1626. Web. *Luminarium.org.*

just a few days, his reputation was ruined.[5] It was no longer possible for Bacon to serve as the lord chancellor of England, and he was also barred from other court positions that suited his expertise and experience. There was little left for him to do except to devote himself to writing. Some historians believe Bacon was the true genius behind the plays of William Shakespeare, but what is known for certain is that he had a profoundly lasting influence on philosophy and science.

On April 9th, 1626, Francis Bacon died of pneumonia.[5] He left behind debts that were much larger than his savings and estate could cover, and thus, he left behind little but a controversial reputation and a series of books. Though Bacon had fallen from the greatest height a person outside the royal family could achieve, his collected writings on the scientific method and organization remained very popular, particularly in England and the British American colonies.

[5] Parris, Matthew and Maguire, Kevin. "Francis Bacon–1621." *Great Parliamentary Scandals.* 2004. [5] "The Broadview Anthology of Seventeenth-Century Prose." 21 March 2001.

Chapter 4 – Marie de Gournay

(1565-1645)

Marie de Gournay did not have many years to spend with Michel de Montaigne, but nevertheless, she became a close friend near the end of his life. She is most famous for her proto-feminist essay on equality for the sexes. Her unconventional lifestyle of writing as a single woman was a complement to the theoretical argument that women and men had equal access to education and public offices. The enormous literary body that is Gournay's work concerns many philosophical questions.

Marie de Gournay was part of a small aristocratic family, in which some of her relations were involved in the legal field while some were authors. When Marie's father purchased the property called Gournay-sur-Aronde when his daughter was still very young, he earned the right to add "de Gournay" to the family name. By keeping that tenuous grasp on the aristocratic fabric of France, Marie's future remained all that much brighter.

An avid reader, Marie taught herself a variety of subjects to make up for the lack of formal higher education that was not provided for her.

Her focus was very much influenced by the leaders of the Renaissance and the emerging leaders of the Enlightenment, and therefore, her studies centered upon classic Latin, Greek, and French literature. Through this personal education, Marie cultivated a deep love of early writers and poets such as Plutarch and Ronsard. For the young student, however, none was more interesting than the essayist Michel de Montaigne.

In 1588, de Gournay had the immense pleasure to meet Montaigne personally, and the two formed a fast friendship. In fact, following their first meeting, de Gournay wrote and published a novel entitled THE PROMENADE OF MONSIEUR DE MONTAIGNE, CONCERNING LOVE IN THE WORK OF PLUTARCH. The book explored the role of women in classic literature and the repercussions of those expectations in the contemporary world. De Gournay expressed the fears of young women, as well as the disappointments of brides, who are often forced to bend to the will of the men in their lives.

De Gournay's friendship with the older essayist grew so great that the latter began to refer to her as his adopted daughter. They shared ideas and conversed about their work regularly, so much so that when Montaigne died a few short years after their meeting, he had already arranged for de Gournay to handle his unpublished works. She even stayed at Montaigne's Bordeaux château for a year after his death to follow through on that responsibility. De Gournay published the new edition of her friend's huge essay collection in 1595, complete with her own preface. In later years, she would continue to release newly edited versions of Montaigne's work, which was as he had intended.

De Gournay lived a precarious and somewhat stressful life in 16th-century Paris after the death of her mentor. As an unmarried woman earning her own living with translations and writing, Marie was often the object of ridicule among her social peers. On the other end of the spectrum, Marie's lifestyle inspired a keen curiosity in some literary circles within and outside of France. She attracted both harsh criticism and judgment, as well as support from women in search of their own form of self-governance.

De Gournay composed her own essays, based largely on the structure and content of those of Montaigne. In her own words, she supported the idea of free will versus predestination; she also pushed for a humanistic educational system that was more heavily rooted in classical works than on scientific treatises. Like Montaigne, de Gournay firmly believed in the fundamental truth and goodness of her religion, and though she did not lament the existence of scientific pursuit, she did not want it entangled with religion.

In 1610, de Gournay famously defended the French Jesuits, who were blamed for the assassination of King Henry IV.[6] Though the assassination was certainly carried out by a Catholic fanatic, it could not be proven that the Catholic Jesuits had organized the murder. Regardless, the attempts of the late king to foster religious tolerance through his Edict of Nantes had failed. Marie de Gournay was well loved by the remaining royal family, however, and she continued to enjoy the patronage of Henry IV's wife and royal consort, Queen Margot. She also maintained friendships with other intellectual women of Europe, including Anna Maria van Schurman and Bathsua Reginald Makin.

Much of de Gournay's work focused on the translation of classic literature, but she also composed poems and essays. The translations won her the most acclaim and patronage, but she persevered as an essayist despite the lower popularity of those manuscripts. In 1634, she published a collection of essays entitled THE SHADOW OF THE DAMOISELLE DE GOURNAY. Like Montaigne, she would edit and rework them several times over the course of the following years.

The Shadow of the Damoiselle de Gournay continued much in the vein of her novel, in that it further questioned the disparate roles of men and women in contemporary society. She examined the formal

---

[6] "Henry IV." *Biography.* Web.

institutionalized systems that kept women from obtaining a good education and a respected career, and she idealized a world in which females could achieve just as much as men.

Her essays also defend the importance of figurative language to communicate complex philosophical truths. Her moral theory, based primarily on France's lack of equality between the sexes, is one in which the future must provide more opportunities to its disenfranchised. Her pioneering gender research was an important part of the Enlightenment in France, spurring on a collection of women throughout France and Europe who pushed frantically for a chance to change the world with their intelligence and hard work.

When Marie de Gournay died in 1645, her essays had already had an amazing effect on French women and men alike. She had cultivated herself into an example of a smart, modern female, capable not only of self-education but of supporting herself through intellectual means without the help of a husband. Her peers and followers would continue to forge onward as the Enlightenment began to pick up speed.

Chapter 5 – René Descartes

(1596-1650)

René Descartes was born in France on March 31st, 1596. Shortly after his birth, his mom died from complications in childbirth, and his father, Joachim, sent Descartes to reside with his grandmother and great uncle. Descartes joined the Jesuit Collège Henry-LeGrand at La Flèche at the age of eleven, where he received his primary education. In 1616, he had earned a *licence* in canon and civil law from the University of Poitiers.[7] After completing his degree in law, he went to Paris to follow a legal profession at the wishes of his father.

Soon after arriving in France's capital city, however, Descartes abandoned any thought of a legal career in favor of travel and worldly knowledge. Descartes soon developed a desire to join the military service, so in 1618, he became a mercenary soldier in the Protestant Dutch States Army in Breda. Undertaking the long-term study of military engineering, the young soldier met and became firm friends with a man who became his teacher, Isaac Beeckman.

---

[7] A *licence* is a degree below a Ph.D. that is given by schools in some countries, particularly those in Europe.

Beeckman was a scientist and a philosopher. In his meetings with Descartes, the pupil showed an eager affinity for mathematics and science. The elder Beeckman taught his student about the growing theory of corpuscularianism, which would eventually lead to a scientific grasp of atomic theory. Beeckman convinced Descartes to focus his studies on mathematics. Working and studying together, the pair decided that they must try to develop a connecting theory to link mathematics to the new science of physics.

Descartes was on deployment in Newcastle on the Danube (also known as Neuburg an der Donau) on a chilly November evening in 1619 when he shut himself alone in a room with a little oven to stay warm. While there, he had a sequence of dreams that led him to believe he had just had a holy vision that helped him connect the various fields of science in which he had been studying. Upon waking, Descartes created analytical geometry and wrote descriptive explanations of how to use it to explain parts of philosophy. From these dreams, he found that the study of mathematics would be a key component in his life, as would the promotion of what he considered to be true knowledge. This momentous occasion solidified Descartes' future reputation as a philosopher.

Descartes tried to use his new techniques to tackle an issue that had been bothering him for some time: false proofs within the scientific method. His personal quest was to find reality without being held back by prejudices, seen or unseen. The process that came of this line of thought came to be called "hyperbolic doubt," since Descartes decided that any theory or supposed law that could be subjected to even a hint of doubt was therefore untrue. This clarification of his previous convictions caused him to think on a variety of subjects, including that of existentialism. In trying to better understand the truth of existence, he finally found that "I exist" is unquestionable and is, therefore, totally certain. From that personal discovery, the philosopher proceeded to confidently ascertain the true existence of God.

In his philosophical treatise of God, published within his book *Meditations on First Philosophy* in 1641, Descartes contemplates what is needed to discern something's existence or truth. The "Causal Adequacy Principle" is used and explained as a balance between the cause of the object and the effect of that same object. According to Descartes, this means that nothing can emerge from anything and that the opposite is also true. It was a tenuous but powerful connection between physics and the inner truths of humanity, just as Descartes had been looking for.

A translation of a passage of *Meditations on First Philosophy* says the following:

> I suppose therefore that all things I see are illusions; I believe that nothing has ever existed of everything my lying memory tells me. I think I have no senses. I believe that body, shape, extension, motion, location are functions. What is there then that can be taken as true? Perhaps only this one thing, that nothing at all is certain.[8]

One of the features of the Renaissance and the Enlightenment was the pervasive use of Latin in place of common languages, at least in terms of written philosophy and research. The original theory behind academia being written and shared only in Latin was pragmatic; since Europe was comprised of so many languages, Latin could be used as the universal language from Ireland to Russia. As the middle classes grew, however, the use of Latin remained only in the hands of the wealthy and highly educated, while working-class people only learned to read in the local vernacular. Descartes, however, wanted his books to be accessible to everyone on equal footing, so, therefore, he chose to write in his native French.

Because of this decision, Descartes' reputation did not only flourish among the highly educated people of France and the rest of Europe, but it was also widely celebrated among the middle-class residents of France as well. Furthermore, having *Meditations* and other books published in French meant that Descartes' ideas became some of the most inspirational and fundamental of the entire Enlightenment era. Methods of thinking, particularly about the realities of human life and existence itself, offered readers a new way to look at themselves and examine their own personalities.

Descartes was one of the most famous philosophers and scientists in Europe after he published *Meditations*. Fascinated by the man and his theories, Queen Christina of Sweden asked Descartes to visit her in 1649 and teach her about his ideas on love. That very winter, Descartes embraced the idea and relocated to Sweden to begin their lessons. Unfortunately, the arrangement was less than ideal since Queen Christina soon tired of her tutor's preoccupation with physical mechanics, making their meetings rather very sporadic. Only a few months later, on February 11th, 1650, Descartes contracted pneumonia and died.

Though the philosopher had lived his entire life as a Catholic, and had always been confident in the existence and goodness of the Catholic image of God, he was buried in a Protestant nation and therefore missed out on the traditional funerary service. The graveyard in which he was buried held mostly orphans. As an even further disservice, considering Descartes' faith and the philosophical inspiration he had been to many of the nations of Europe, Pope Alexander VII added all of Descartes' work to the List of Prohibited Books in 1663.[9]

---

[8] Descartes, Rene. *Meditations on First Philosophy.* 1641.
[9] Brenden. "Descartes' Meditations." *There It Is.* Web. 2014.

Chapter 6 – Bathsua Makin

(c. 1600-c. 1675)

Bathsua Makin was born around 1600 in England, and though little information remains to clarify her life in detail, her role as a teacher helped cultivate an entire generation of female scholars. Her own father, Henry Reginald, was a schoolteacher in Stepney, a small borough outside of London, England. It was quite possibly his influence on Bathsua that led her toward a life of learning and teaching in her own right. Her perseverance in learning a wide variety of languages and pursuing a teaching career earned her the moniker of England's Most Learned Lady.

Makin's specialty was in languages, and she learned to read and write in all Europe's most prolific tongues. By 1640, she was made tutor to the children of King Charles I, the most prominent position a woman—or a tutor—could hold in England. The court of Charles I was Anglican, as England had broken from the Catholic Church nearly a century earlier during the reign of King Henry VIII. Makin herself was most likely also an Anglican, a reformed religion that was closer to Protestantism than to the old Catholic traditions. While Makin ran lessons for the royal children and taught them how to enunciate in various languages, the king's status was in imminent danger.

Charles I was not a popular king, and because of this, his Catholic detractors believed they stood a chance at overthrowing his crown. Catholic sects in Britain had been waiting for such an opportunity ever since the Reformation, and several times before, coups had been attempted. The difference this time was that it would be successful. Furthermore, the organizers of the coup had the support of the largest and most powerful entity in Europe: The Catholic Church.

The 17th century was a very dangerous time for people to question the Catholic Church, which had essentially ruled over them since the Romans transitioned from being worshippers of ancient deities into Christians. Western Christianity was a significant element in the preservation of classical culture after the collapse of the Western Roman Empire in the 5th century, and it was seen by millions as the guiding rule of the land.[10] Members of the Church set up convents and trained missionaries to convert early European cultures, which stretched from Rome as far as Ireland, into Christians. The eastern part of the Roman Empire metamorphosed into the Byzantine Empire, in which Christianity was also at the heart of the culture. England and many other regions of Europe had embraced a form of Protestant Christianity by the 1600s, but monarchs and their followers were still not safe from the ongoing Catholic Inquisition. By the time the Enlightenment washed over Europe, Catholicism was still a very integral part of the nations in Europe.

When Charles I was deposed and executed in 1649 in favor of a government headed by Oliver Cromwell, Charles' children were taken into the custody of Cromwell's trusted supporters. For Bathsua, who felt a strong sense of responsibility toward the children in her care, there was no choice but to stay with her ward, Princess Elisabeth Stuart. Bathsua followed the girl, performing her

---

[10] "The Fall of Rome." *BBC*. Web.

duties faithfully until the princess died in custody almost two years later. Promised a pension for her services but never receiving pay, the distraught Makin made her way back home.

She looked once more for tutoring jobs, which were still plentiful, given her credentials and her proven dedication to the children in her care. She helped many aristocratic children master their vernacular, as well as any other European languages they may have fancied learning. During the years she passed preparing lessons and watching her students grow in mind and body, Charles II was instated to the throne of England in place of his father. The political landscape of the country was far from settled, but Bathsua survived the worst of it and came out on top.

In Tottenham High Cross in 1673, Makin and an associate founded a school dedicated to the education of society women. Located just a few miles outside of London, the school's governess was Makin herself. She instructed the students in traditional female topics such as music and singing, but she also taught advanced English, Latin, and French. For girls who wanted to push their language lessons even further, Makin also offered lessons in Greek, Hebrew, Italian, and Spanish.

The following excerpt is from Makin's "An Essay to Revive the Ancient Education of Gentlewomen," published in 1673.

> The Barbarous custom to breed Women low, is grown general amongst us, and hath prevailed so far, that it is verily believed (especially amongst a sort of debauched Sots) that Women are not endued with such Reason, as Men; nor capable of improvement by Education, as they are. It is lookt upon as a monstrous thing; to pretend the contrary. A Learned Woman is thought to be a Comet, that bodes Mischief, whenever it appears.

> To offer to the World the liberal Education of Women is to deface the Image of God in Man, it will make Women so

high, and men so low, like Fire in the House-top, it will set the whole world in a Flame.[11]

This essay, a spiteful work in which the author expresses her anger at the fact that women are considered of lesser intellect than men, was Makin's legacy to the world. Even though the intricate details of her own life have been lost, this essay still survives.

---

[11] Makin, Bathsua. "An Essay to Revive the Ancient Education of Gentlewomen." 1673.

Chapter 7 – Anna Maria van Schurman

(1607–1678)

Anna Maria van Schurman was a very bright and curious woman, and she enjoyed the full support of her family to pursue as much education as possible. In 1634, she received an invitation from the University of Utrecht to write a poem in Latin for their grand opening. She complied, and the subsequent poem put forth her ideas on the rights of women to study and to be educated. In 1641, this work was expanded into an essay and then translated into English in 1659 under the title "The Learned Maid." Two years later, at the age of 29, she received another invitation from the university: this time, she was asked to become a student.

She accepted, making van Schurman the first woman in the Netherlands (and perhaps in all of Europe) to become a university student. It was unheard of for any female, regardless of her nobility, to attend university in the 17th century, but van Schurman's famed intellect and her influential family helped her earn that privilege.

While seated behind a curtain in class so as not to distract the male students, Anna Maria earned her law degree.

Schurman also learned to speak in fourteen languages and was able to read and write in many of them as well. She could communicate in Latin, Greek, Hebrew, Italian, French, Arabic, Persian, Ethiopian, German, and Dutch, to name just a few. She was equally adept in art, music, and literature, and she also pursued higher knowledge of medicine, philosophy, and theology. Accomplished in geography, mathematics, and astronomy, Schurman's education was every bit as diverse and in-depth as those of her male counterparts.

Schurman was not only dedicated to her studies of science and philosophy but also to her belief in God. She used her elevated position in society to question the official stance of European nations on the education of females. While certainly controversial, she won many people to her cause by linking education to being a good Christian. As one's religious faith was still the most important achievement in life during the Enlightenment, men and women of all stations were happy to accept the notion of women's education when it was linked to piety. In fact, Schurman purported that women of noble birth were obligated to achieve scholarly achievements as part of becoming better Christians and to help grow their love for God. This stance actually helped many male scholars embrace the idea of female education.

There were few learned women at the time, so those who were had a natural desire to connect with each other. Anne de Rohan-Chabot, Antoinette Bourignon, Dorothy Moore, Princess Elisabeth of Bohemia, and Queen Ludwika Maria of Poland (also known as Marie Louise Gonzaga) were among the educated women corresponding with Schurman during her lifetime. One of her closest friends was a friend of the family, Marie du Moulin.

The women corresponded in many languages, including the ubiquitous Latin. While connecting with educated women and advocating the education of women, van Schurman was just as connected to the most educated and cutting-edge thinkers as were her male counterparts, thanks in great part to her Famille d'Alliance. The Alliance sprung forth among Schurman and her female friends from the need to have a support network. The men had the Republic of Letters, as too did many of these women, but without the primary encouragement of the Alliance, the women of the Enlightenment may not have had the confidence to take part in the plethora of written conversations that would move Europe into the modern age.

One of van Schurman's most famous correspondences was with René Descartes, the man often referred to as the first modern philosopher. Descartes and van Schurman disagreed on their interpretations of the Bible and had lengthy dialogues on the subject.

Anna Maria van Schurman wrote extensively on the subjects that interested her, and much of her work was actually published. Between 1639 and 1673, van Schurman published "On the End of Life," "The Star of Utrecht," and "Choosing the Better Part." Many of these essays, in particular, "The Star of Utrecht," were reprinted several times over the course of the 17th century due to their high popularity.

Not only was van Schurman a thinker and a writer whose ideas were somewhat radical and unacceptable to many people of the time, but she was also an inspiration for some. Johan van Beverwijck, a Dutch doctor, wanted to dedicate one of his publications to van Schurman and congratulate her for her role in the changing views of European society. The problem for van Schurman was that she held her Famille d'Alliance up as a whole movement, one in which the individual was only a small part. She did not want to receive individual attention for her work because she believed it would detract from the group as a whole. She also worried about criticism, which could be incredibly harsh concerning the ambitions of women. She wrote to the doctor, pleading that he refrain from naming her in his book.

The following is an excerpt from her letter:

I have seen your treatise, most Illustrious Man, which you entitled *On the Excellence of the Female Sex*. Beware, then...particularly since you have raised so many examples of illustrious women to such an exalted peak of renown that you might seem to have discussed them more for the purpose of ill-will than for the purpose of emulation...Therefore...I vehemently implore you, nay rather by the faith of our inviolable friendship I do solemnly beseech you, do not persist...in dedicating this book to me.[12]

Though Doctor van Beverwijck had only meant to congratulate Anna Maria van Schurman, she took it upon herself to explain in detail what harm his book's dedication may cause. In that same letter, she told her admirer how it was common among many men to only believe that the rare woman was capable of thoughts as complex as their own. Those men were loath to accept that all women were capable of the very same achievements under the right circumstances and instead merely acknowledged the merits of a handful of females. To prevent this, van Schurman explained that she did not under any circumstances want to be singled out for her achievements apart from her female peers.

Nevertheless, Anna Maria did find relative fame within the intelligentsia of Europe. She was bequeathed the nickname "Minerva," in honor of the Roman goddess of wisdom, the arts, commerce, and political warfare. True to the moniker, she was indeed an accomplished artist as well as a learned woman. She studied engraving and made very intricate engravings in wax and on glass, wood, and ivory. She painted portraits and was documented as being the first Dutch painter to use pastels in portraiture. She was

---

[12] Pal, C., *Republic of Women: Rethinking the Republic of Letters in the Seventeenth Century,* Cambridge University Press 2012

even given an honorary position in an art guild in 1643, which was another rare accomplishment for a woman at the time.[13]

Later in life, van Schurman's deep religious beliefs led her to encounter some disillusionment with the Church and to seek the ideas of the Reformation. She took up the cause of the Labadists, who followed the ideals of the French priest Jean de Labadie. Labadie had been renounced by the Catholic Church and even the Dutch Reformed Church, but perhaps it was his poor reputation with the largest church of the region that gave him more influence among those who were disillusioned by it.

The Labadists were a religious movement of the Protestants, and Labadie's orthodox Christian religion concentrated on personal religious dedication than Christian doctrine and theology. Van Schurman became one of Labadie's main followers in the mid-17th century and became so active within the new church that Labadie's followers called her "Mama." She wrote pamphlets and essays on their behalf, one of which formally announced her break with the Dutch Reformed Church in 1669. It was called *On the Reformation necessary at present in the Church of Christ.*

Her outspokenness against the largest gathering of Protestants in the Netherlands angered many people there, and van Schurman was forced to relocate along with dozens of other Labadists. She accepted an invitation from her friend Princess Elisabeth of Bohemia and took up residence in the Duchy of Saxony. She lived there until Labadie's death in 1674 and then returned to the Netherlands.[14] Her own final years were spent living with others on a shared property,

---

[13] Bohn, B. & Saslow, J.M., *A Companion to Renaissance and Baroque Art*, Wiley & Sons 2012

[14] "Jean de Labadie." *Encyclopedia Britannica.* Web.

in keeping with the Labadist doctrine, and her lifestyle was non-materialistic. She died in 1678.[15]

---

[15] Larsen, Anne R. *Anna Maria Van Schurman, 'The Star of Utrecht': The Educational Vision and Reception of a Savante. 2014.*

Chapter 8 – Dorothy Moore

(1612-1664)

Dorothy Moore was born to a family of some standing in Ireland. Her father, John King, was knighted and granted a lease on an estate and then went on to hold several political positions. Dorothy's brothers received an excellent early education and went on to attend Cambridge. Dorothy, on the other hand, received what she later called a basic noblewoman's curriculum.

Later in life, Moore wrote a short treatise on girls' education, lamenting the regrettable learning she had received due to her gender. She detailed how a girl could come away from her lessons having only learned how to dance and how to fill the mind with needless, unprofitable, and prideful things.[16]

As was the typical way for girls at that time, Dorothy's education was not extensive and ended fairly early. Once she had learned to dance, sew, and manage a home, marriage was the next step for her. Dorothy married Arthur Moore, the son of Sir Garrett Moore, the Earl of Drogheda. The couple had three sons, in whose education Dorothy took a firm hand. In searching out the best tutors and

---

[16] Pal, C. *Republic of Women,* Cambridge University Press 2012

lecturers, the young mother began to communicate with many people, including Anna Maria van Schurman, Bathsua Makin, John Dury, and Samuel Hartlib.

In the 1630s, Bathsua Makin wrote, "I have heard about you, my beloved friend, honourable Lady, and I am happy and joyous for the one goodness that Heaven has borne us in our days, to renew the glory of your people."[17]

Dorothy Moore never stopped learning, despite the feeble education she had received in her youth, and she mastered many languages such as Hebrew, Greek, French, and Latin. She had studied the work of René Descartes, as did most philosophical students of the time, and then moved on to other writings and began to correspond with others in the same pursuit.

She was extremely interested in religious study, and she aimed much of that study toward the role of women within the Church. She had considered moving into a position of authority with the Church, such as a preacher in a religious community that believed women could perform such work as well as men.

In 1639, Johan van Beverwijck published a book he had written extolling the intellect of women and putting forth the idea that women could have abilities equal to men. One of the examples he used to support his ideas was Dorothy Moore:

> The widow of an English nobleman, not yet twenty-seven years of age, adorned with all the graces of body and soul. In a short time she learned Italian and French to such an extent that she could read works written in both languages and spoke French fluently. This encouraged her to study Latin, which she also mastered soon. Not stopping there, she embarked on the study of Hebrew, in which she progressed so far in a few months that she could read the Bible in that

[17] Van Dijk, S., "I Have Heard About You" Foreign Women's Writing Crossing the Dutch Border, Uitgeverij Verloren, 2004

language. In addition she is so devout that, in between her studies, she sets aside a special time each day to spend piously, reading and meditating.[18]

In a letter Moore wrote to Katharine Boyle in 1643, she said,

> I conceive every Member of Christ ought to propose unto themselves as their Duty without excluding our Sex... many are apt to think us all together incapable of such service as I now speak off, but until you can prove us incapable of that honor of being Members of that body I must believe that every Member in his owne station may be profitable to the rest.[19]

In her never-ending quest to secure full education for her children, Dorothy reached out to John Dury in Holland after the death of her husband. John Dury was the son of Robert Durie, who was a Scottish Presbyterian who had been exiled for attending an assembly the king had prohibited. John Dury was brought up in Holland, where his father had gone after he had been exiled. John was dedicated to the peaceful unification of Protestants throughout Europe. He worked and wrote extensively on this and published *Concerning the Work of Peace Ecclesiastical* in 1641.

Dury helped Moore secure a top-rated education for her sons, and she brought them to Utrecht in 1641. She was going to take a position as a governess to Queen Elisabeth of Bohemia's children. This position did not come to fruition, however, as Moore was thought ineligible when she and Dury planned to marry. Engaged or married women were still not thought suitable for such positions. Dorothy did not at first seek to remarry, but in the end, she was convinced that she and Dury would be able to do more of God's work as a married couple. In that work, Dorothy continued to pursue

---

[18] Barry, C., *Irish Philosophy*, Irishphilosophy.com web.

[19] Pal, C. Republic of Women, Cambridge University Press 2012

the opportunities for women within the Church, as well as work on the reformation of the Church.

Moore, at times, corresponded with André Rivet, a French Huguenot theologian who at the time was an influential member of the faculty at Leiden University in the Netherlands. In these letters, Moore talks about the capacity of women to serve and asks that they should be allowed to serve the public based on their capacity to do so rather than on their sex. She tells Rivet that women are incorporated into Christ the same as men are and that their goals to serve should be considered in the same way. Her correspondence with Rivet was quite intense and helped to further develop her ideas when it came to the vocations of women within the Church.

Dorothy Moore wrote extensively to those she thought could help in her work to achieve the realization of women being allowed to hold a vocation within the Church. She took great risks in this communication and was thought of as quite radical by many. Moore's convictions as to the suitability of women to serve society based on their abilities rather than their sex, as well as their abilities to be educated the same as men, were the basis of most of her writings.

Chapter 9 – Princess Elisabeth of Bohemia

(1618-1680)

Princess Elisabeth of Bohemia, also known as Princess Elisabeth of the Palatinate, was the oldest daughter of Elizabeth Stuart and Frederick V, who was the elector of Palatine. Her father served as the king of Bohemia for a short time before moving to the Netherlands in exile; Elisabeth joined her parents there at the age of nine. In 1633, Elisabeth received an offer of marriage from the king of Poland, Władysław IV Vasa.[20] It was an arrangement that would have helped her family's situation, but the girl refused because the king was Catholic. Instead of changing her Calvinist faith, which was of the utmost importance to her, Elisabeth chose to enter a nunnery.

In 1667, seven years after joining the nunnery, Elisabeth became the abbess of the convent. This authoritative role allowed her to extend the care that was offered by herself and the women of the institution to many religious refugees who were flooding into the country,

---

[20] Lascano, Marcy. *The Cambridge Descartes Lexicon.* 2015.

particularly from France. She knew firsthand what it felt like to be cast out of one's birth home due to politics and religion. Hers was a particularly unique viewpoint, as she was a Calvinist in a Lutheran convent. She knew that if the Lutherans could take her in that she should extend the same offer to helpless people of various belief systems, including those of the Labadist faith.

Princess Elisabeth of Bohemia is most renowned for her extended correspondence with René Descartes, and actually, her existing philosophical texts are these letters. In one letter, Elisabeth insists Descartes further explain his theory on the relationships between material objects, namely the chance of their causal interactions and their associations. These letters also discuss the physics of Descartes and the essence and balance of individual liberty of will.

Elisabeth and Descartes' letter-writing campaign began with Elisabeth questioning how Descartes chose to describe the capacity of an intangible object to use a concrete object. In this original question, the discord between flesh and brain is the core of the problem. As Elisabeth saw it, the mind was more likely to influence the flesh rather than the other way around. In view of the causal effectiveness of an immaterial mind, Elisabeth suggested that Descartes should attempt to articulate the causes of the interactions between the mind and the body.

They also discussed politics together in great detail. Descartes devoted his *Principles of Philosophy* to Elisabeth, and due to her suggestion, he composed *The Passions of the Soul*. Although it is important to understand Descartes' opinions by studying this interchange, it is equally important to note that Princess Elisabeth challenged her friend's beliefs. They discussed the English Civil War and the potential of the people to reinstate their ancient monarchy. She was greatly saddened by the religious divisions in England and hoped to help the war-affected Protestant English as best she could in her capacity as abbess of the Herford convent.

Elisabeth also corresponded with Anna Maria van Schurman, who inspired her to study history, physics, and astronomy. Van Schurman was a mentor of sorts to Elisabeth, accepting her into the Famille d'Alliance, a group in which other women had found comfort and knowledge amongst one another. Elisabeth became a central feature in women's intellectual circles.

Elisabeth didn't limit her correspondence only to René Descartes and the women of the Famille d'Alliance; she also exchanged letters with members of the Quaker religious sect. The Quakers had emerged in England following the Civil War, and though their beliefs were generally based on Christianity, they also believed that God existed inside each person. Robert Barclay and William Penn were two such believers with whom Princess Elisabeth shared letters, and though their attempts to convert her were wasted, their alternative theories interested her greatly. The princess was endlessly interested in the various worldviews around her, and she participated rigorously in the Republic of Letters in order to obtain as much information as possible.

Given the unique situation in which Elisabeth found herself, it makes sense that her interests turned not only to theology and truth but to political theory as well. The interest of Elisabeth in assessing political events in detail was directly linked to her hope that one day she and her family might be placed back into a position of power where Catholic armies could not dethrone them. Unfortunately, such a thing was not possible, and Elisabeth died at the convent in 1680.[21] Her series of intelligent letters remained an inspiration to the women of the Enlightenment and beyond, and they helped contribute to the proof that females were much more than the roles they had been assigned by history.

---

[21] Goldstone, Nancy. *Daughters of the Winter Queen: Four Remarkable Sisters, the Crown of Bohemia, and the Enduring Legacy of Mary, Queen of Scots.* 2018.

Chapter 10 – Robert Boyle

(1627-1691)

Robert Boyle was an Irishman whose family was involved in the political protests against the English. Due to the ongoing violence between the two sides, young Robert was sent away from home until the violence between the Irish Catholics and the Protestants passed. It was in 1644, after the death of his father, that Boyle returned to England, where he had attended the prestigious Eton College. He was a highly educated young man who had already traveled Europe extensively and stayed in Florence to study the works of the elderly and house-arrested astronomer Galileo Galilei. Within a few years after inheriting his father's Irish estate, Boyle returned to his birthplace to pursue a career in science. Unfortunately, he found it difficult to obtain the necessary equipment in his native home, and he also expressed his displeasure at the lack of intellectual camaraderie he found there. He persevered for several years before returning to England and immersing himself in the bustling scientific community that was there.

Boyle's personal studies and original work concentrated on ethics and rhetoric—the first focusing on morality and the second on persuasive writing and speech. As he matured, however, Boyle found himself surrounded by a variety of natural philosophers and became interested in pursuing similar topics as his friends instead of French literature. In the 1650s, he started to spend time with the Hartlib Circle, a group of intellectuals that focused on Samuel Hartlib, a German polymath. Some educational researchers, whose jobs fascinated Robert Boyle, were among the representatives of the Hartlib Circle.

Hartlib himself was a highly educated person of German descent, and in the mid-17th century, he emigrated to England. He was an advocate of various scientific topics—including agriculture, botany, medicine, finance, and alchemy—and he designed improvements to many mechanical inventions, including Blaise Pascal's mechanical calculator. From between around 1640 to 1660, Hartlib established a European network of scientific letters and patents, and this network was often known as the Hartlib Circle. The network included specialists in all areas of science, and these were individuals like Robert Boyle, the horticulturalist John Beale, and the physicist William Rand. The Hartlib Circle was dedicated as much to higher education as it was to Protestantism, and therefore, an entire section of the letter-writing network was committed to spreading and safeguarding such theology.

Robert Boyle's role within the Hartlib Circle was primarily that of a chemist. Boyle regularly experimented with gases, often alongside his colleague, Robert Hooke. Together, the pair constructed an air pump to aid in their experiments, and subsequently, Boyle published *New Experiments Physico-Mechanical, Touching the Spring of the Air and Its Effects* in 1660. Using the air pump, Boyle noticed that as the pressure of a gas grew higher, the volume of that gas shrank. This relationship between gas volume and pressure became known as Boyle's law.

To explain the conclusions of his own experiments, Boyle imagined gas as a collection of tiny particles—a theoretical model known at the time as corpuscularianism. The science of lens-making had advanced leaps and bounds from the invention of the telescope and the microscope a century earlier, but these instruments still did not have the magnification power necessary to reveal cellular structures or the smallest of microparticles. Corpuscularianism, therefore, was heavily based on conjecture and, to a lesser extent, experimental results.

As per his book, Boyle subscribed to a mechanical philosophy of the universe. Also called mechanism, this philosophy regards reality in the same vein as clockwork; that is, it operates under a strict set of rules that can be determined via careful research and experimentation. At the time, mechanism was primarily concerned with weeding out un-scientific methods and pieces of data from the scientific field, which proved to be quite a cumbersome undertaking. Nevertheless, such methodology was the utmost desire of the era's best scientists, and through painstaking observations and publications, Robert Boyle was able to contribute a great deal of high-quality information to the world.

Boyle's belief in the existence of atoms was not universally shared, but thanks to his friendship with Samuel Hartlib, it was given due respect within the network. The fact it was given any respect at all was probably largely due to the support received by scientists and peers within the Hartlib Circle, something which defined the Enlightenment and differentiated it from the more secretive, anxiety-ridden earlier days of the Scientific Revolution. Though Boyle's predecessors, such as Galileo Galilei and Giordano Bruno, had often suffered for their scientific revelations or had to keep their works from publication altogether, the scientists of the Enlightenment felt less pressure to adhere to the Aristotelian beliefs of the Catholic Church.

The positive influence of the Hartlib Circle upon science was twofold: first, the network of great minds provided intellectual support; secondly, the circle's Protestant foundation helped move a great deal of power and authority away from the Catholic pope and the Catholic Inquisition. With Protestant churches focused primarily on their own rights of existence than on any particular field of science, the relationship between burgeoning non-Catholicism and new-wave science was reciprocal.

For Robert Boyle, affiliation with the Hartlib Circle meant that he had significantly less to worry about in terms of religious or political punishment than had Galileo. Therefore, he pushed ahead with his experiments and atomic theory, influencing a great number of contemporary and future scientists. Boyle's insistence that the scientific method—such as that described by Francis Bacon—was crucial in the field was echoed by many of his colleagues.

Furthermore, Boyle and the other members of the Hartlib Circle benefited from the regularity and solidarity of their group, as the countries of Europe were constantly at war with themselves or others. Letter writing within the Hartlib Circle was not only a way for scientists and philosophers to keep up to date on discoveries and methodology, but it was also a way to acknowledge the lasting loyalty and non-partisanship of its members.

Chapter 11– John Locke

(1632-1704)

John Locke was an Englishman whose early education was in London at Westminster School beginning in 1647. His studies included languages (Latin, Greek, Hebrew, and Arabic), geography, and mathematics. By 1650, John Locke was given the honor of being elected "King's Scholar." The financial boost from this title allowed him to buy many more books for his library, including Greek and Roman classics. He was a bright student but did not enjoy school and would later write *Some Thoughts Concerning Education* in 1693, in which he suggests there are better ways to educate young men and states that private tutoring would be better.

In 1652, Locke began his education in medicine at Oxford. Again, Locke was a good student but found the confines of formal education somewhat lacking. He read the works of Francis Bacon and René Descartes on his own since they were not part of his education at Oxford. After he graduated in 1656, Locke pursued this new kind of science fully, and soon, he himself came to be seen as a philosopher, one who, in the 17th century, laid out the foundations for "Western philosophy." Locke became an influential man in that realm, and he wrote extensively on the topic. As a major contributor to the development of new philosophical thought, he was one of the first empiricists, a person who holds the belief that all knowledge came from experience obtained through the senses.

Locke's work also advanced the theories of knowledge and what it really meant. He studied and wrote about epistemology, which is the study of what the differences are between beliefs and opinions. Locke did put forward the idea that there were no innate ideas or morals that were present in the minds of humans when they were born. He believed those came only from the observations and reflections of the mind and that knowledge was only gained through the connections of the mind to ideas through such observation.

John Locke has been called the "Father of Liberalism." Liberalism holds that a person's liberty should be at the center of political organizations. Freedoms such as the freedom of choice and an individual's right to be equal in the eyes of the law made up the main premise that defined early liberalism and helped to drive the further development of that political philosophy.

Locke had a strong effect on the thoughts of liberal policy as a major philosopher and political theorist. He refused to believe in the idea that kings held a divine right to rule over others, and he argued that every person was endowed with the rights to life, liberty, and property. If a king failed to uphold those rights, the people were more than in the right to remove them from power. As such, Locke played a leading role in the revolutions of the United States and France, similar to the roles Thomas Jefferson, James Madison, and Voltaire played. Much of that influence was related to Locke's ongoing theories of social contracts.

The concept of a social contract concerns the relationships between people in a community. The personal and professional duties of each person, according to the supporters of the social contract theory, depend on the agreements made between all of the people, spoken or unspoken. The nobility in a classic European kingdom, for example, had a social contract with their monarch to provide armies and taxes. In return, the monarch had a responsibility to provide protection for those citizens from other nations and armies. Social contracts were described by Plato back in the 5th century BC, and modern versions of social contracts were conceived by Thomas Hobbes before John Locke produced his own variant.

Another fundamental part of Locke's beliefs was the state of human nature. According to Locke, the natural state in which mankind exists includes complete personal freedom to live as one pleases without being imposed upon by others. Locke did not think that living in one's natural state meant that you could do anything you felt like. According to Locke, nature is characterized by liberty, but it is not a condition without ethics or social judgments and punishments. Locke's theory of humankind's state of nature is that it predates politics and government, but it holds to what he believed are fundamental human morals.

Although Locke believed in the freedom of religion, he was strongly against the Roman Catholic Church's claim that their pope was infallible, as it was unprovable. He believed the Catholic Church was a threat to English autonomy and the freedom of the Protestants. Even Locke's idea of freedom of religion had its limitations. For example, while he believed that people had the freedom to follow any religion, he did not believe they also had the right to be atheists.

The matter of property and ownership was of great importance to Locke's theories of personal freedoms, and those ideas were furthered later by 19th-century thinkers. Property is a central thesis of his philosophical writings, including the property of one's own body. He argued that each person owns his or her own body and that one's physical self cannot be used without express permission. At a time when slavery was still a large part of the economic fabric of Europe and the Americas, such words were powerful.

As far as obtaining property outside of one's own body, Locke believed that such a thing could be done through the output of labor.

Labor, combined with material objects, equated to property in the form of crops, clothing, and whatever products are created by one's work. Locke's viewpoint that the harvest belonged to the field workers was a precursor to labor theories touted by Karl Marx and Friedrich Engels.

John Locke's writing on political philosophy influenced the Scottish Enlightenment in the 18th century, where his work was built upon by the next round of political thinkers and writers. Locke's work was also an influence on the writings of both Voltaire and Jean-Jacques Rousseau, who contributed more thoughts on the rights and liberties of citizens within society.

Locke's most known works are *An Essay Concerning Human Understanding* written in 1689 and his *Two Treatises of Government*, also published in 1689. In the first, he put forward his theories on human knowledge being based on experience, and in the second book, Locke put forward his ideas that political organization was built on the individual rights and freedoms of the people and their consent to be governed.

Locke's work (as well as Voltaire's and Rousseau's) were sources of major inspiration for the American revolutionaries, who mirrored his theory in the writing of the United States Declaration of Independence in 1776. John Locke was an advocate of what was later established in the government of the United States: the separation of executive, legislative, and judicial powers. His political and philosophical ideas remain strongly influential in the Western world, centered upon the main tenets of freedom, knowledge, and challenging authority.

Chapter 12 – Isaac Newton

(1642-1726)

Isaac Newton was very young when he first began to formulate his masterful scientific theories. When he was out of Trinity College, Cambridge, for eighteen months due to an outbreak of plague, Newton stayed at home and worked on many of these ideas. Young and somewhat prideful about his scientific discoveries, Newton liked to regale audiences and friends with the story of how, one day while sitting in his garden and contemplating the universe, an apple fell from a tree nearby and struck the ground, perfectly exemplifying the law of gravity. This incident became a central feature of his long-term study of gravity and physics.

In 1687, Newton explained his three laws of motion in the book *Philosophiæ Naturalis Principia Mathematica*.

1. Every object persists in its state of rest or in uniform motion until it is compelled to change that state by forces impressed on it.

2. Force is equal to the change in momentum per change in time. For a constant mass, Force equals Mass times Acceleration (F=ma).

3. For every action, there is an equal and opposite reaction.

It would be many years before the revelations Isaac Newton had during his absence from school would be published for posterity. They were included in the pages of *Philosophiæ Naturalis Principia Mathematica*, which was released to the public in 1687. Known colloquially as *Principia*, the book was an oddity for one particular reason. The book was written in the vernacular of Newton and his scientific colleagues—there were no simplified summaries or metaphors included to pander to the lesser educated.

Though it was quite common practice for intellectuals to write their manuscripts in Latin, a language only understood by wealthy families of Europe who could afford the best education, it was also customary to publish secondary versions of such books in the local vernacular. Newton would not do so until 1728 when *Principia* came out in English as *Mathematical Principles of Natural Philosophy*.

As it was, only members of the Royal Society of London and their international colleagues of similar esteem were capable of understanding the complicated terminology of *Principia*. Though this may seem like a callous move on Newton's part, there may be a good explanation for his failure to address the common people in a way they could relate to. The days of the intensive Catholic Inquisition were not that far behind Newton, and indeed, the Inquisition was still technically in effect during the 17th and 18th centuries. Being an astute man, Newton probably realized that if members of the clergy could not understand his work, they would have much less reason to persecute it.

Newton's book has been described as an introduction to the field of physics and rational mechanics. Rational mechanics, in Newton's own words,

> …will be the sciences of motion resulting from any forces whatsoever, and of the forces required to produce any motion, accurately proposed and demonstrated…And therefore we offer this work as mathematical principles of his

philosophy. For all the difficulty of philosophy seems to consist in this—from the phenomenas of motions to investigate the forces of Nature, and then from these forces to demonstrate the other phenomena...

Principia was divided into three separate books, or sections. The first of these sections addresses the potential movements of physical bodies when under no opposing forces, such as gravity. These movements would theoretically take place in a full vacuum. The second section discusses the movements of the same physical objects while under the influence of other forces, thereby attempting to explain the characteristics of those forces. The last section of the book examines the specific interpretations of the data concerning planetary and satellite movements.

Newton's first law of motion states that a body in motion maintains the same movement unless an external force acts upon it. Similarly, unless a force moves on it, it remains this same way. Every moving object in space will travel at the same speed in a straight line, including planets. For instance, the planets are going straight ahead, but the gravity of the sun is attracting them to it. It is this force of gravity that causes the moving planets to move around the sun in roughly circular orbits. For billions of years, they have been circling the sun because other forces have been too weak to significantly change their movements.

In Newton's second law of motion, an item speeds up to the quantity of power that acts on it. When no strength affects the object, its speed remains unchanged. Constant acceleration is required to move the planets around the sun. However, here, acceleration means "change of direction" instead of the "change of speed." The gravitational force of the sun constantly changes the route of a planet as it circles the sun but never directly bends it toward the sun.

The third law of motion says that for every action, there is an opposite action of equal force. For example, if you stand on a small boat and walk off the edge, the boat moves backward just as you move forward. In the same way, the sun feels the force of the planets, but because the sun is so much larger than the planets, it has little effect on the movement of the sun.

Principia astounded the scientific communities in England and abroad, and it earned Newton invitations to every salon, café, and science club in Europe. His work would become fundamental to the entire future of physics.

Chapter 13 – England's Civil War

(1642-1651)

Enlightenment values did not just lend themselves to furthering science and other knowledge but also to the establishment of fair and equal societies for the benefit of every person. In England and Scotland, many people believed that to achieve such a society would ultimately come at the cost of the monarchy. It took decades for that idea to find the right timing; Queen Elizabeth I had done her part to unite the ancient foes that were England and Scotland by leaving her kingdom to the Scottish king, her own cousin, James Stuart.

After taking over control of the Scottish government in 1567, James VI became used to having virtual free reign over Scotland; however, this was not to be the case in governing England, which had much of the power in the hands of the parliamentarians. Upon inheriting the English throne in 1603, James I, as he was known once he inherited the English crown, soon learned that the extent of his political power there was nothing compared to his power in Scotland. Nevertheless, he was a peaceful man who did not seek to shake off these laws and simply rule with an iron fist. Although he did rack up quite a large personal debt, his reign was largely unwrought with hardships. The same could not be said of his son, King Charles I.

Charles I was not a popular figure among his subjects. In 1625, he married a Roman Catholic French princess, Henrietta Maria, which was most unbecoming of the ruler of a famously Protestant nation. Francis Bacon was very much set against the marriage, insisting, unsuccessfully, that Charles wed a princess from one of the Protestant neighboring kingdoms. A marriage to one of the Spanish Hapsburg princesses was also seriously considered in an attempt to align Spain and England on positive terms. The king was not to be deterred, however, and so, Charles married Henrietta Maria, the daughter of Bourbon King Henry IV of France, one year before he was crowned king of England and Ireland, and separately, the king of Scotland.

Charles I believed in the divine right of kings, the same doctrine held by his fellow European monarchs, which meant that these kings had been appointed to their positions by God. Believing this, Charles' frustration at the continual criticisms of Parliament had a simple solution: get rid of Parliament. They weren't necessary under the divine right; only Charles was necessary to rule his lands according to it. In 1629, he stripped all the parliamentarians of their office. For over an entire decade, the king governed without a public advisory body, a period of history that was termed the Personal Rule, or the Eleven Years' Tyranny.

The unpopularity of the young king was not to be abated, as he soon tried to revive an archaic ship tax. This tax had been levied intermittently throughout the history of England, but the members of England's inland counties had never had to pay it during the centuries of its existence. The ship tax, or ship money as it is sometimes referred to, required coastal counties to provide the monarch with a certain number of ships or pay an equivalent tax in exchange for a strong naval defense. Charles I stated that the same amount should be paid by all of England's regions, regardless of whether they touched the sea. England's Parliament would surely have rejected the taxation, but it was implemented to the great grief of Charles' people.

Charles insisted that those who did not pay the tax should be punished, no matter their rank, and this lowered him further in the eyes of the nobility. At the time, it was considered inappropriate to subject members of the nobility to the same types of fines and punishments as commoners. However, without Parliament, the king could not easily obtain the money he needed to implement various plans since it had been Parliament's job to agree upon taxation schemes and levy them. For this reason, Charles I relied on the ship tax and other medieval forms of taxation that had been forgotten within English or Scottish law. He even dug up an ancient law that required any man who had made more than £40 per year to serve the Crown as a knight, which would serve his army in defense of the persecuted French Protestants, called Huguenots.

By 1640, Charles I was broke and completely without money with which to govern, thanks to his dismissal of Parliament. So, he decided to appoint a brand-new Parliament that included the soon-to-be infamous Oliver Cromwell. With the government back in action once again, the king focused on revamping the Church of England, as well as the Church of Scotland. Neither population was excited to embrace change, though, the first having only a century earlier been subjected to the Reformation of King Henry VIII.

Charles I was not convinced at the longevity of the existing form of religion in his realm, however, and he worried about the schism between Catholics and Protestants. He believed that the answer was to make further concessions to Catholics within the existing Church of England doctrine, such as those which had been stripped away purposefully by Queen Elizabeth I before Charles' father took the throne. Specifically, the king supported what he called high Anglicanism, a sacramental version of the Church of England in which some of the ceremonies of Catholicism was given back to the reformed religion.

Again, this was a highly controversial idea. Charles I's father had written the King James Bible in an attempt to further unify the people of England and Scotland under one faith, but the outliers and nonconformists remained high in number. Charles I decided to appease them by implementing his own interpretation of religion, which began with making the Church of England more formal in nature. Charles' representative, the Archbishop of Canterbury, William Laud, exchanged the wooden communion tables of the churches with stone altars resembling those of a cathedral. The move seemed like a return to Catholicism to many, and they protested vehemently.

Scotland revolted first, beginning the Bishops' Wars in 1639 as its clergy attempted to oust Charles I's choices for bishop. Scotland had already been extremely unhappy to be given the new king's version of the Book of Common Prayer, which was rewritten as high Anglican. Parliament began to take control away from the king, and led by Oliver Cromwell and Robert Devereux, the Earl of Essex, defectors strove to abolish the monarchy completely. A series of conflicts occurred over the following years, but Charles did not openly declare war until August of 1642.

Cromwell's Parliamentarians ultimately defeated Charles, who was forced to surrender to enemy forces in 1646, ending the First English Civil War. The war flared up again in 1648, as Charles, who was still being held prisoner, attempted to make pacts with outside forces and turn the tide of the war in his favor. Ultimately, the fallen king was tried for treason and found guilty in 1649, ending the Second English Civil War. Parliament had him beheaded in front of White Hall Palace that same year, though his body was ceremonially buried in St. George's Chapel at Windsor. England, Ireland, and Scotland had effectively abolished the monarchy, leaving Parliament—mostly Oliver Cromwell—in charge.

Charles II, the heir to his father's throne, was henceforth considered to be the new king by the Royalists; though, officially speaking, he was denounced in 1651 during the Third English Civil War, which was the final civil war that ended later that same year. Kept safe throughout the course of the civil war, Charles II would eventually be reinstated as king of Scotland, England, and Ireland in 1660 following the downfall of Cromwell and a swell of support for the fallen monarchy. Constitutionally speaking, the outcome of the English Civil War was that future monarchs were not allowed to govern without the express consent of Parliament. It changed what would become the British Empire forever.

Chapter 14 – The Royal Society of London

1660

The same year that Charles II was crowned king again, the College for the Promoting of Physico-Mathematical Experimental Learning was founded in England. This lengthy title would eventually be changed to the Royal Society of London, and its founders were Isaac Newton, Robert Hooke, and a handful of other natural philosophers based in England. It had been many years in the making, and the final piece of the puzzle was an endorsement from the reigning monarch. The group was not interested in pursuing the cause of many other Republicans who continued to seek a monarchy-free state; instead, they bet their future on the power of the reinstated royal family to remain at the head of the English government.

According to the Society, which remains the oldest national scientific organization in the world, the purpose of the club was multifaceted. The various roles of the Society were (and still are) to encourage research, recognize scientific achievements, support scientific excellence, guide policies, and foster collaboration and education. These principles were extended to include Britain's many colonial landholdings and later to the Commonwealth nations under the Crown.

John Wallis, an eminent Society mathematician, wrote the following about the formation of the organization.

> About the year 1645, while I lived in London (at a time when, by our civil wars, academical studies were much interrupted in both our Universities)...I had the opportunity of being acquainted with divers worthy persons, inquisitive natural philosophy, and other parts of human learning; and particularly of what hath been called the New Philosophy or Experimental Philosophy. We did by agreements, divers of us, meet weekly in London on a certain day and hour, under a certain penalty, and a weekly contribution for the charge of experiments, with certain rules agreed amongst us, to treat and discourse of such affairs...

> About the year 1648-49, some of our company being removed to Oxford (first Dr. Wilkins, then I, and soon after Dr. Goddard) our company divided. Those in London continued to meet there as before (and we with them, when we had occasion to be there, and those of us at Oxford...and divers others, continued such meetings in Oxford, and brought those Studies into fashion there.[22]

By the winter of 1661, the participants in both locations discussed the title of the company and how a royal charter of association would be obtained. Diplomatic meetings with the king's advisors moved the plan forward with few problems, and the Charter of Incorporation was impressed with the Great Seal of the Realm on July 15th, 1662. From then on, the Royal Society of London officially existed as an organization with the full support of the king. Charles II was appointed as the founding officer of the Royal Society of London for the Improvement of Natural Knowledge. A second royal charter was signed on April 23rd, 1663, and the Society has maintained the official support of all subsequent British monarchs since then.[23]

Lord William Brouncker served as the first president of the Royal Society. In compliance with a collection of laws and standing orders, the Society was organized to be regulated by its council, headed by the elected president. The members of the council and the president, who were (and still are) chosen by standing members, remain at the administrative heart of the Royal Society to this day. Soon after receiving their royal charter, the group started its own journal, *Philosophical Transactions of the Royal Society*. It is currently the oldest scientific journal in existence, and its issues became a regular part of the Republic of Letters.

Scientific experimentation was a primary focus of the Royal Society in those first few years of existence, and the chemist Robert Hooke managed most of those. Hooke's work on these experiments encompassed a wide variety of burgeoning sciences, including optics, astronomy, and biology. Hans Lippershey's first telescope was invented just eight years after the formal formation of the Society, after which Hooke was inundated with requests to peer more closely at various parts of the Earth and the stars. His experiments revealed some of the first microorganisms and showed the rotations of Mars and Jupiter. Hooke's 1665 book *Micrographia* detailed experiments using a microscope to examine fossil remains, which led him to make early hypotheses about biological evolution.

The Society conversed heavily about the possibility of establishing its own educational college. Prior to 1666, they used a building at Gresham College in London for their meeting place, but the campus was temporarily made unavailable after the Great Fire of London swept through the city. The group moved to Arundel House

[22] "History of the Royal Society of London." *Royal Society Web.*
[23] *"Prince of Wales opens Royal Society's refurbished building." The Royal Society. 7 July 2004.*

afterward, and during 1667, the members of the Royal Society made fervent strides toward creating its own campus. They held meetings, collected funds, and drew up plans for the buildings, which would include member and guest housing and potentially even a library and a chapel. Enthusiasm for the project soon faded, however, and in 1673, the Society moved back into Gresham College.[24]

In the 17th century, the Royal Society boasted memberships from some of England's and Europe's most famous and inventive people, including Isaac Newton, Christopher Wren, William Cavendish, Antonie van Leeuwenhoek, and Robert Boyle. It was an era of incredible scientific growth in England, and the influential reach of the Society continued on throughout the rest of the European Enlightenment.

The group's motto is *Nullius in verba*: Take nobody's word for it.

---

[24] Tinniswood, Adrian. *The Royal Society.* 2019.

Chapter 15 – Marie du Moulin

(1622-1699)

Marie du Moulin was a Dutch writer and scholar whose participation in the Republic of Letters is indicative of a much larger circle of professional and intellectual women within the group. Though not much is known about du Moulin, including details of her birth and large sections of her adulthood, historians have uncovered the fact that she was the daughter of the famous French theologian Pierre du Moulin.

Pierre was a professor at the French universities of Leiden and Sedan, and apart from Marie, he fathered at least seventeen other children. As one of the older siblings, Marie was responsible for much of the care of her sizeable young family, but she also found adequate time to pursue her schooling. Like her father, she was interested in theological debates, and beginning in young adulthood, she immersed herself in the company of others who valued such discourse.

In 1633, Marie du Moulin moved from France to the Hague in the Netherlands to stay with her aunt, whom she was named after. The elder Marie was married to André Rivet, another well-known theologian of the day. Rivet was also a French Huguenot, which was a Protestantism sect that was fairly popular in that part of Europe.

During the 17th century, the French Huguenots were heavily persecuted in Roman Catholic France, which explains why many such as Rivet—and eventually Marie du Moulin—emigrated to Protestant-friendly Dutch lands.

In the company of her aunt and uncle and their friends, Marie was inspired to take on further studies to expand her own knowledge. She became a woman of many languages, famously learning to read and write in Hebrew. During her twenty years with the Rivet household, du Moulin made friendships with men and women such as Anna Maria van Schurman, Pierre Bayle, and Valentin Conrart, all of whom had the shared goal of constant self-improvement. Marie, her uncle, and many of their shared friends wrote and exchanged mail within the Republic of Letters.

Her position as a Protestant located outside of the stronghold of Catholic Europe meant that Marie du Moulin had the chance to participate in theological discussions without the fear of political repercussions. She even took part in one such conversation between Rivet, van Schurman, and other family friends one day when they philosophized over the famous story of Joan d'Arc, better known in English as Joan of Arc.

A firm hero in Catholic France, 15th-century Joan of Arc believed that she had been contacted by the Archangel Michael, St. Margaret, and St. Catherine of Alexandria in a series of visions. The young girl's belief in the truth of these visions led her to demand a meeting with French Dauphin Charles VII in order to offer her assistance in his war against English rule. Amazingly, King Charles VII was convinced by the girl's story and sent Joan as part of the relief army to the battlefield at Orléans. The fighting at Orléans ended just nine days after the arrival of the relief army, a sign which many in the French court took as proof that Joan was on a mission from God. A string of wins on the battlefield soon led to the long-awaited coronation of Charles VII as king of France.

Du Moulin and her friends debated a number of supposed facts related to the story of Joan of Arc and King Charles VII, including whether her talents were best placed on the battlefields of the 100 Years' War. Both van Schurman and du Moulin argued that the young girl, formerly so isolated on her family farm, should have turned to study and academics instead of war. That way, they insisted, Joan could have avoided being martyred at the hands of the contemptuous English and further served her cause, as she would have had her whole life to right the wrongs against France.

The Joan of Arc debate may seem pedestrian to a modern philosopher, but to a group of 17th-century Frenchmen and women under the constant threat of the Catholic Inquisition, questioning the merits of a religious martyr was cause for imprisonment, if not death. Though not as bloody as it had been in previous centuries, the Inquisition was still hard at work weeding out so-called heretics from the Catholics in France and Spain, and life was simply not safe for people who wanted to explore other religious ideas.

Du Moulin went back to France in 1655 to look after her aging father for the duration of his remaining years. Following her father's death in 1658, Marie bought the family home and lived there with her cousin, Pierre Jurieu. Pierre was a professor at the University of Sedan, but this institution was shut in 1681 as a part of a series of closures affecting Huguenot organizations. Fearful for their safety, Marie and Pierre left France once more for the Netherlands. There, Pierre secured another professorship at a college in Rotterdam.

In 1683, the city council of Haarlem contacted Marie du Moulin and asked her to be the director of a new boarding school for daughters of noble Huguenots who had fled from France. Though du Moulin would only hold this position until 1686, her time at the school was inspiring. She found that she could help and support entire classes of girls and young women all at once and thereby change the course of the future.

When she returned to France in 1686, du Moulin was arrested as a Huguenot. She was imprisoned and then taken to a monastery for young Catholics. She escaped, however, and fled to the Netherlands once more. Finding herself in the Hague once again, she became the director of a boarding house founded by the Princess of Orange, who was soon to become Queen Mary II of England, and was placed once more in charge of female Protestant refugees from France. Her lessons and guidance at the boarding school were unquestionably formative to an entire generation of women whose lives may otherwise have ended painfully.

Marie du Moulin stayed at the school for the rest of her life, passing away in 1699.

Chapter 16 – Conflict in the Royal Society

(1668-1669)

The Enlightenment was indeed a time of improved science and ethics, but the scientists within the Royal Society of London were by no means free from their human egos. Several times over the course of the Society's long history, arguments have sprung up between members or between members and invited guests. One such feud occurred early on in the life of the Royal Society, and it was between two of its most famous members: Robert Hooke and Isaac Newton.

The problem began as soon as Newton presented his first scientific paper to the Society in 1672.[25] His appearance at the Society helped to solidify his reputation as an excellent mathematician and fledgling scientist. One man was less than impressed, however, and that was Robert Hooke, an original member of the Society. The problem was that Newton had made some hypotheses about optics, and Hooke—whose profession was in optics—believed these to be incorrect.

Newton claimed that light was comprised of seven colors within its spectrum and that these were made of particles. Hooke, however,

---

[25] Moiz, Aimah. "Bitter Rivals, Hooke Versus Newton." *Spectra Magazine.* 2018.

firmly believed that light was not comprised of particles but that it was a wave. Hooke was not alone in his beliefs, but he does seem to have been the only member of the Society to take Newton's paper personally. The two began an exchange of letters to hash out many of the details in both of their work, many of which Newton took little time to address.

The following letter is one of the first Newton wrote in response to Hooke's criticisms.

> June 11th 1672
>
> Sir
>
> I have sent you my Answers to Mr Hook and P. Pardies, wch I hope will bring with ym yt satisfaction wch I promised. And as there is nothing in Mr Hooks Considerations wth wch I am not well content, so I presume there is as little in mine wch he can except against, since you will easily see that I have industriously avoided ye intermixing of oblique and glancing expression in my discourse...
>
> Your Servant
>
> I. Newton[26]

John Collins, mathematician and member of the Royal Society from 1667 until his death in 1683, wrote the following about the matter:

> Mr Hooke moreover affirmed coram multis that in the yeare 1664 he made a little Tube of about an Inch long, to put in his fobb, which performes more than any Tellescope of 50 foot long made after the common manner; but the Plague happening, which caused his absence, and the fire, whence redounded profitable employments about the Citty, he neglected to prosecute the same, being unwilling the Glasse grinders should know any thing of the Secret, Gottignies the

---

[26] "Newton's Reply to Hooke and the Theory of Colours." *The University of Chicago Press Journals.* 1963.

Scholar of Gregory of St Vincent, whose remaines he hath, is said to have made wonderfull (but in what respect I know not) Tellescopes at Rome, and to have published a Treatise of Dioptricks there.[27]

With this note, Collins reveals how Robert Hooke reacted to Newton's instructions concerning the manufacture of a modern telescope. Hooke claimed that the tube of the telescope did not have to be six feet long, as Newton recommended, since he himself had once invented one that was only one inch in length that apparently worked better than any of the large telescopes he had used since. The tiny telescope had not been reported to the scientific community, however, because a plague had hit the city, and there was also a fire later on. Besides that, Hooke said that he did not want to reveal his secrets to local glassmakers.

Isaac Newton and Robert Hooke never spoke rudely to one another, at least in their letters, but their tense relationship was well known. After Newton was admitted to the Royal Society soon after his first appearance there, the pair continued to argue over the apparent characteristics of light. Nearly every invention or theory Newton presented, Hooke saw fit to discredit or devalue it in some way, often claiming to have made similar statements prior to Newton, particularly after the latter submitted the first drafts of his later book *Opticks* to the Society.

While Hooke wasn't the only one who disagreed with the idea of light as a particle, he was alone in the professional attacks against Newton. Newton defended his research vigorously and submitted his work directly to *Philosophical Transactions of the Royal Society*. It did nothing to resolve the conflict, though, and Newton threatened to leave the Royal Society in March of 1673, sick of having his work so harshly criticized by a fellow member.

Newton remained popular within the Society, however, as well as with the public. Friends in the Society spoke to him soothingly about

---

[27] Ibid.

the tension and convinced him to stay the course with them. Three years later, in 1676, Hooke mocked Newton again, accusing him publicly of plagiarizing his own work concerning the properties of light. For the next few years, the two men continued their rivalry through an endless exchange of violent letters until Newton had had enough in 1678. Apparently suffering from a psychiatric breakdown, the famous scientist retired from public life and sought out a more peaceful pastime.

The feud, however, was far from over. When Hooke told his fellow Society members that he had solved the mathematical relationship between two celestial bodies in 1684, he failed to deliver the proof, although he did have a concise idea. Eager to have the numbers worked out, astronomer Edmund Halley visited Isaac Newton and asked if he might be able to solve it. Newton responded that he had already done so but had lost the papers. He set to work right away to put the numbers back together.

Halley himself financed the publication of these equations, which were a major part of Newton's groundbreaking book, *Philosophiæ* NATURALIS PRINCIPIA MATHEMATICA. People who could understand the book were astounded at Newton's ability to put together working mathematical equations to explain the laws of motion better than Kepler had already done. However, once more, Robert Hooke had a problem. According to Hooke, the mathematical equations Newton had used to define part of the relationship between celestial bodies had been copied from his own work.

Hooke told the members of the Royal Society that Newton had stolen his theory of the reverse square law to explain the physics in his book, arguing that without his own work, there would be no *Principia*. Although Newton had made sure to thank his colleagues in the notes of his book, including Hooke, for all their help and input, he was adamant that he had done his own math. He considered canceling the printing of the last part of the book, but Halley convinced him that it would be a grave error.

Hooke and Newton never properly reconciled their differences, and the tension between them continued until Hooke's death in 1703. Ironically, Newton returned to the Society to serve as its president immediately after his antagonist had passed away.

Chapter 17 – Charles-Louis de Secondat (Montesquieu)

(1689-1755)

Charles-Louis de Secondat, the Baron de La Brède et de Montesquieu (known to history simply as Montesquieu), was a French judge and a philosopher on the subject of politics. Born in 1689, Montesquieu was heavily influenced by England's Glorious Revolution and the subsequent union of England and Scotland as one kingdom. These events would influence him to participate in politics and help shape the fundamental structure of future republican governments, including that of his own country.

Montesquieu initially began a career as a lawyer after earning his law degree at the University of Bordeaux. By 1708, he moved to Paris to find work and stayed there for several years until the death of his father in 1713. Upon his return to Château de la Brède, Montesquieu married the daughter of a rich Protestant family, providing himself both with a wife and a large dowry. A few years afterward, his uncle endowed him with another large sum. These windfalls of money allowed Montesquieu to reconsider his law career, and he ultimately decided to retire in favor of studying the sciences and writing books.

He succeeded in the literary world by publishing his first book, *Persian Letters*, in 1721; it was a satire in which two fictional Persians take a trip to Paris. Before leaving home, the older tourist puts his multiple wives in the care of his slave eunuchs. While away from home, the two men correspond regularly with people in Persia, and through their letters, we see a fascinating picture of Western culture, highly contrasted with that of the Islamic world. Politics are discussed frequently, including a sharp satirical reference to John Law's system. John Law, a Scottish economist in the same vein as Adam Smith, believed that a nation's wealth lay in trade, not currency.

Persian Letters was not meant to be a novel, Montesquieu later explained, but it gained a huge following throughout Europe as just that. In fact, the book serves as a primary example of what is today termed an epistolary novel, which is a collection of letters. Thanks to the great success of the book, its author was able to continue his career as a writer.

About ten years later, in 1734, Montesquieu released *Considerations about the causes and the greatness of the Romans and their Decline* in 1734. The book was markedly different than his first publication, as it was not satirical but a culmination of careful historical research. Originally, *Considerations* was only meant to be a brief essay on the writer's chosen subject, but Montesquieu found the topic to be inexhaustible. The first published edition contained 277 pages, and it covered a detailed history of the Roman Republic and Empire starting in 753 BCE with the founding of Rome and stopping in 1453 with the fall of Constantinople.

Though *Considerations* was altogether different from the book that introduced Montesquieu to literary Europe, it received even more attention and is considered a masterpiece by many. Within its pages, Montesquieu asserts that Rome's fundamental policies of wealth, expansion, and naval power were the source of the Roman Empire's great success and the eventual cause of its downfall. He believed that over time, the power of the empire deprived its citizens of a sense of civic pride and duty, and he notes a constant downturn of general morality, both in Rome's citizens and its leaders, that was only lifted periodically due to the excellent leadership of emperors like Marcus Aurelius.

The book was an ideal addition to the European repository, particularly given the importance accorded to the Greco-Roman educational system during the Enlightenment. It had begun during the Renaissance and would continue for a few more centuries in the educational facilities of Europe's wealthiest and most influential families. Europeans had an unquestionable thirst to understand all they could about the people whose civilization they considered part of their own shared history. Consequently, Montesquieu's writing career was a huge success.

His next project would be even more critically acclaimed than his previous books. Released anonymously in 1748, it was called *The Spirit of the Laws*. Just three years after its publication, the book was put on the List of Prohibited Books by the Catholic Church. Indeed, it included some highly controversial subjects, including a basic reorganization of state power.

Montesquieu asserted that the cultural and demographic elements of a group of people must be taken into consideration in order to rule effectively. Specifically, he advocated a constitutional government system in which the various roles of government were separated from one another. This, he argued, would also depend on the preservation of personal freedoms, which included the abolition of slavery. Using the term "political liberty" to describe his ideal political system, Montesquieu was compelled to explain that his theories required society to let go of two common misconceptions concerning liberties. The first is the idea that liberty is the same thing as democracy; the second is that liberty means doing anything you want.

The book fascinated audiences, and despite being banned soon after publication, *The Spirit of the Laws* put a crucial idea into the minds of Enlightenment thinkers: the organization of governments into several branches so that each could be performed optimally. Separating government into branches, such as into the branches of federal, legislative, and municipal, would divide power and therefore prevent corruption.

Montesquieu traveled extensively throughout Europe, spending time in Austria and Hungary for several years while writing many books and essays and searching for relevant study materials. He also lived for a year in Italy and a year and a half in England, where his ideas were greatly appreciated in the post-civil war kingdom with no loyalty owed to the Catholic Church. In England, he joined the society of Freemasons, which was considered to be an eminent group of intellectuals and political leaders. Eventually, however, in poor health and blind, the famous writer returned to France. He died there in 1755, at the age of 66, having suffered a short illness with a high fever.

Though he was gone halfway through the century, Montesquieu's ideas of equality, separation of government, and an end to slavery lived on, proving to be particularly inspiring to the French, as well as the American colony of the British that was all the way on the other side of the Atlantic Ocean.

Chapter 18 – Social Reforms and Workhouses

(1700 onward)

Samuel Hartlib and his famous circle had advocated for improvements to be made for the poorer people of Europe. One of the particular projects Hartlib championed was that of the workhouse, a place he imagined would provide occupation, shelter, and basic amenities to Europe's homeless and otherwise hopeless residents.

Welfare laws in most of Europe were grossly lacking. The workhouse had its roots in the desire of the government and its rulers to remove beggars and vagabonds from the metropolitan landscapes. There were clusters of bridewells—prisons for minor offenses—in England by the 1690s.

Central governments in Denmark started changing their ideas about aid, unemployment, and corrective labor. The attempts to change these social problems were not entirely successful, however. The Odense foundation document states categorically that its purpose was "to frighten all those who enjoy vagrancy and dissolute behavior, and repel them from a province where they risk losing their liberty, and where the authorities will endeavor with all the means at their disposal to force them to do that which they most of all dislike, namely to earn their own bread and subsistence by means of honest work…"[28]

In early modern Denmark, neither the central government nor local authorities seemed to have had the resources or the will to examine the fundamental factors and types of antisocial behavior, vagrancy, and petty crime until the later years of the Enlightenment. Three workhouses were built in the cities of Amsterdam, Nieuwe Pekela, and Middleburgh. It was acknowledged by many that these institutions, in general, were unsuccessful, complaining about the prospective corruption of kids in particular, but were seemingly unable to enforce the required institutional change. In neighboring Belgium, there were five workhouses in as many cities by 1777.

For most cities and smaller parishes, the workhouse would not make a significant cultural impression until the Victorian era. It was championed most intently in Britain, where Queen Victoria responded to rampant homelessness and poverty in her realm by updating the kingdom's ancient Poor Laws, which had been put in place as early as the 14th century and had been further revised by the Tudors and successive monarchs. In fact, the new Poor Laws were enacted in 1834 by Victoria's grandfather, King William IV, but they would have a huge impact on Victoria's over 63-year reign.

Before the 1834 enactment, caring for the poor of the kingdom fell to the parish priests, who collected taxes from the nobility and doled it out as they saw fit. Unfortunately, by the 17th and 18th centuries, during which the Enlightenment took place, there were more unemployed and homeless people than these parishes could handle, and the nobility was firmly set against any tax hikes for the purposes of caring for the poor. This system of care was in drastic need of an overhaul, and as far as Britain was concerned, the future of that system would center on the workhouse.

---

[28] H. Chr. Johansen. *Naering og bystyr*. 1983.

Parishes remained in charge of decisions concerning the care of the poor, but in the late 18th century, more and more of them started building their own localized workhouses to which members of villages and families without work prospects could be sent. Though superficially these places were advertised as providing care to those who were most in need, others were of the opinion that the workhouses were made out to be terrifying and dreary so as to motivate the poor to occupy themselves in other jobs. Since all men, women, and children were registered at their local workhouse if they were found sleeping on the streets or begging for money, the only way to leave the workhouse was to find employment elsewhere. For women, that often meant prostitution or domestic service; for men, it was common for them to attempt to be sent to prison in order to escape the long hours of tedious work. Otherwise, attempts to escape were usually punished harshly, particularly for the children who were often orphans and had nowhere else to go, as far as the state was concerned.

The people supporting the new Poor Laws thought it would decrease the price of care for the needy and promote self-sustenance by those housed in such facilities. Such facilities were equipped with residential services, including places to sleep and eat, but their main focus was to bring in able-bodied adults and children to perform a variety of tasks. The revamped Poor Laws were meant to ensure that every person without a job, home, or both would be accommodated within a local workhouse, where food, shelter, and a small salary would be provided in exchange for long days of work. There would be some education for children that joined the workhouse, but they, as well as adults, had to work every day.

The work coincided with the increasing commercialization of large British cities like London and Manchester, where factories had sprung up so that masses of employees could manufacture basic items like thread, rope, textiles, and cutlery. They also attended to laborious work like crushing rocks for building materials and crushing bones for fertilizer. As the Industrial Age moved forward, more of the work was done with dangerous machines, which caused many injuries and deaths.

Though the able-bodied were put to work, the workhouses were still responsible for providing food and housing for the sick and infirm members of society who had no other means to survive. Many of them had separate sections within the large, undecorated building for the ill and old. In addition to the men's infirmary and the women's infirmary, there were segregated quarters for able-bodied workers, as well as for boys and girls between the ages of seven and fifteen. Another area housed the children under the age of seven. Not even married couples were allowed to break the segregation rules since it was considered a good practice to prevent the poor from having more babies.

According to legislation, workhouses throughout Britain were to be comprised of a dormitory, lavatory, workrooms, hospital, mortuary, bakery, receiving area, dining hall, and church. Usually, there was little space to spare. Rooms were made as small as possible to accommodate the necessary components of the workhouse; as many as eight rooms might be built into a space of only 16 feet, or there might be 32 adults placed in a dormitory that was 20 feet in length.[29]

According to the laws, inmates of the workhouses all over Britain were to be awoken at 5 a.m. and attend church by 6 a.m. Following prayers, they were offered breakfast until 7 a.m., after which point, they were set to work until noon. The second meal of the day arrived at noon, and workers and inmates had one hour to eat, and that was followed by another stretch of work that lasted until 6 p.m. Before workers could retire for the day, they were required to attend another church service that lasted until 7 p.m. At 7 p.m., dinner was scheduled for one hour, after which everyone was free to return to their dormitories.

According to Edwin Chadwick, a workhouse inspector who became focused on improving the welfare of the people he found there, inmates would simply sit and do nothing between dinner and bedtime at 8 p.m. They had no forms of entertainment and no room in which to carry out any leisure, meaning that the simple act of sitting or lying down was often the only relief after a long day at work. Though there were small outdoor spaces adjoining the workhouses, these were just as crowded and lacking in features as were the dormitories.

Chadwick was horrified by what he witnessed in the workhouses of Britain, and he became determined to force a change in management to provide better conditions for those in the facilities.

> Of the 43,000 cases of widowhood, and 112,000 cases of orphanage relieved from the poor rates in England and Wales, it appears that the greatest proportion of the deaths of heads of families occurred from…removable causes…The expense of public drainage, of supplies of water laid on in houses, and the removal of all refuse…would be a financial gain…as it would reduce the cast of sickness and premature death.[30]

In 1863, the Dihlstrom workhouse in Stockholm, Sweden, had 414 residents. As for Norway, the city of Bergen had constructed an exclusive women-only workhouse, ostensibly for the purpose of helping poor females stay away from the prostitution industry. The Vieb'ltegaard in Svendborg, Denmark, was formerly the workhouse in town; it now contains a marine archive. Ladegården Copenhagen was the hospital of conflict (1733-1767), the mental hospital (1768-1833), and after 1833, a workshop.

---

[29] Bloy, Dr. Marjorie. "Conditions in the workhouse." *The Peel Web.*
[30] Chadwick, Edwin. *The Sanitary Condition of the Labouring Population.* 1842.

Chapter 19 – Benjamin Franklin

(1706-1790)

Benjamin Franklin has been referred to as the "First American." In 1753, after many years as postmaster in Philadelphia, he was appointed to postmaster general for the British colonies, he was the first American Postmaster General during the American Revolution. He worked in public relations, as well as colonial, government, domestic, and international affairs. He was the governor of Pennsylvania between 1785 and 1788, and he was originally the owner and dealer of slaves, but by the late 1750s, he was one of the most prominent abolitionists in the American colonies. Benjamin Franklin is well known for being a polymath as well as one of the driving forces behind the American Enlightenment.

Franklin was born to a family of tradespeople, and he was the tenth child among seventeen children. The Franklins made soap and lamps, but one of his brothers learned the printing trade at a young age, and eventually, Benjamin was sent to apprentice under him. Under his brother James, he began learning the printing trade from the age of twelve.

Spending only ten years in school, the young Franklin mastered the printer's trade between 1718 and 1723, and it was something he took a great deal of pride in for the rest of his life. Wishing to possess the talent to contribute to those endlessly popular pages of print that he worked with, Franklin studied constantly and focused his efforts on learning to write flawless prose.

Like many of his future peers, Franklin discovered that composing competent written work was a singular and lucrative skill in the 18th century. In November 1724, he moved to London to find work producing writing or perhaps working in a printing shop. During his time there, Franklin penned a pamphlet called *A Dissertation on Liberty and Necessity, Pleasure and Pain.* In his paper, Franklin argued that if God is indeed all-powerful and humanity has no real power over itself, individuals could not be blamed for their actions.

The following is an excerpt from that pamphlet:

SECT. I. Of Liberty and Necessity.

I. *There is said to be a* First Mover, *who is called* GOD, *Maker of the Universe.*

II. *He is said to be all-wise, all-good, and all powerful.*

These two Propositions being allow'd and asserted by People of almost every Sect and Opinion; I have here suppos'd them granted, and laid them down as the Foundation of my Argument; What follows then, being a Chain of

Consequences truly drawn from them, will stand or fall as they are true or false.

III. *If He is all-good, whatsoever He doth must be good.*

IV. *If He is all-wise, whatsoever He doth must be wise...*

It will be said, perhaps, that *God permits evil Actions to be done, for* wise *Ends and Purposes.* But this Objection destroys itself; for whatever an infinitely good God hath wise

Ends in suffering to *be*, must be good, is thereby made good, and cannot be otherwise.[31]

Years later, Franklin is said to have hated that particular piece of writing and destroyed all the copies he could get ahold of. Just a year after publishing the work, he returned to the British American colonies and accepted a shop job in Philadelphia. He was only twenty years old when his shop partner died, so, Franklin created another partnership and opened his own printing business.

Franklin and his new partner's earliest achievement was to be granted the role of printing the paper currency for Pennsylvania. Thanks to Franklin's assertiveness, the company also became the currency printer for New Jersey, Delaware, and Maryland. In between contracts, Franklin continued writing articles and essays, publishing them himself. In 1729, he published *A Modest Enquiry into the Nature and Necessity of Paper Currency*. He also championed and published *The Pennsylvania Gazette* that same year, which was soon considered to be one of the best colonial journals in circulation. *The Poor Richard Almanac* was his next big success, released each year between 1732 and 1757.[32]

Franklin prospered, despite making a few inevitable mistakes in business. In possession of enough money to begin lending money with interest and making property investments in the seaside colonies and the British West Indies, he began amassing a great deal of money. He also made partnerships with several other successful publishers throughout the colonies and became one of the richest men in the American colonies. He was one of the richest settlers in the northern portion of the North American mainland by the early 1740s.[33] Philadelphia remained Franklin's home for some decades, and during his time there, he championed various literary, intellectual, and city groups, including the Leather Apron Club, the

[31] Franklin, Benjamin. "A dissertation on liberty and necessity." 1725.
[32] "Benjamin Franklin." *Encyclopedia Britannica*. Web.
[33] Ibid.

Library Company of Philadelphia, and the American Philosophical Society.

He was also a member of the local Freemasons and had a hand in the organization of a Philadelphia police force. His work with the local people sparked a concern in him for the wellbeing of the many poor people struggling to find a steady income or a place to live. He wrote extensively on this subject, as well as philosophy. In 1766, the following excerpt appeared in *On the Price of Corn, and Management of the Poor*:

> I am for doing good to the poor, but...I think the best way of doing good to the poor, is not making them easy in poverty, but leading or driving them out of it. I observed...that the more public provisions were made for the poor, the less they provided for themselves, and of course became poorer. And, on the contrary, the less was done for them, the more they did for themselves, and became richer.[34]

In other words, Franklin believed in helping the poor by giving them jobs and opportunities, not by placing money freely in their hands. He referenced the workhouses of Europe, stating that the uncomfortable state of such facilities ought to properly motivate the poor to find work for themselves, instead of suffering for a pittance for someone else's profit. Humans were motivated by two things, he said: avoiding pain and being taken care of by someone else. God, however, in Franklin's mind, had created such pain to teach the lessons that people needed to know in order to take care of their own selves.

Having retired from work in the 1740s, Franklin spent his time performing experiments with electricity and on writing. He wrote *Experiments and Observations on Electricity*, for which he became internationally famous. Over the next decade, he picked up several public service positions, including city clerk and his aforementioned

---

[34] Franklin, Benjamin. "On the price of corn and management of the poor." *The London Chronicle.* 1766.

position as postmaster general. His healthy interest in science was put in second place behind his sense of public duty, and for that reason, he was an obvious choice for the 1757 trip to London, England, in an effort to have the colony of Pennsylvania made into a royal province. The efforts were fruitless, but since Franklin was a famous personality, he had the opportunity to meet many of London's own famous names, including David Hume.

An adoring British citizen and a staunch royalist, Franklin would be surprised to find himself a member of the Founding Fathers of the independent United States of America. It was warily that he embraced such a role, and throughout the process of the American Revolution, he maintained a personal respect for Britain and great contemporary minds like Hume, whose own philosophies of human nature Franklin must have found quite satisfying.

Chapter 20 – David Hume

(1711-1776)

David Hume was a Scottish-born philosopher, historian, and writer whose works on the subject of empiricism and skepticism would become highly influential. Born in 1711 to an aristocratic family with the name "Home," Hume grew up in Edinburgh and was mostly raised by his mother after the untimely death of his father. Though his family had a respectable name in Scotland, Hume had very little family money with which to sustain himself, and therefore, it was clear to him from a young age that he would need to cultivate a paying career for himself.

At a young age, probably between ten and twelve, Hume joined the University of Edinburgh. The usual age for new students at the university at the time was fourteen, so Hume's academic record prior to enrollment there must have been quite spectacular. All the same, Hume was not an eager student, believing that he could learn the same subjects from books and skip over the patronization of the university's professors. Having told his family that he would pursue a degree in law, Hume instead discovered a passion for literature and philosophy. Unimpressed with the university's structure of learning, Hume left without a degree.

The idea of becoming a lawyer or politician pushed far behind him, Hume changed his career focus to better align with his own personal interests. Determined to make a name for himself in philosophy and other sciences, David Home changed the spelling of his Scottish surname to match its pronunciation, hoping that this would make him more approachable in England.

At the age of eighteen, Hume had an epiphany of which he would never publicly share the full details, but it caused him to devote the next ten years of his life to reading and writing. He committed himself so fully to this path that it is said his mental health suffered to the point of him having a near mental breakdown. According to the philosopher himself, the sickness began with a nearly year-long chill, after which he developed the tell-tale signs of scurvy. A doctor diagnosed Hume's condition as the "Disease of the Learned," though he may have done so as a joke.

Hume's case would not be the first nor the last case of illness—both mentally and physically—to affect a person whose entire waking life was spent within the pages of books or lost in the complex matters of existentialism. This condition, which is marked by a deep depression, put Hume's first great work in danger of incompletion. Yet he persevered, and in 1739, he published *A Treatise of Human Nature*.

The book introduced Europeans to some of the author's complex theories concerning the human state of mind and reality. In the pages of his manuscript, Hume argues that our thoughts are formed from simple impressions, which means that all of our cognitive data must be derived from our own experiences through the senses. Hume recognizes, therefore, that the scientific idea of empiricism must be employed to best accommodate the field of philosophy. Empiricism, in scientific terms, refers to a collection of data gained through experiments and research; in philosophy, it is a method of data-gathering derived from the sensory experiences of humans. It is one of several points of view on epistemology, a field that strives to separate common beliefs from real truths.

Hume believed that philosophy was a science of human nature, subject to the same rules as mathematics or biology. He attempted to explain how the mind operates when collecting and compiling data by using the scientific method proposed by Sir Isaac Newton. Ultimately, he concluded that there was no way to construct a solid theoretical model of reality since the only data available was based purely on human experience, which may lay outside of reality.

In *An Enquiry Concerning Human Understanding*, published in 1748, he wrote:

> Where am I, or what? From what causes do I derive my existence, and to what condition shall I return? ... I am confounded with all these questions, and begin to fancy myself in the most deplorable condition imaginable, environed with the deepest darkness, and utterly deprived of the use of every member and faculty.

> Most fortunately it happens, that since Reason is incapable of dispelling these clouds, Nature herself suffices to that purpose, and cures me of this philosophical melancholy and delirium, either by relaxing this bent of mind, or by some avocation, and lively impression of my senses, which obliterate all these chimeras. I dine, I play a game of backgammon, I converse, and am merry with my friends. And when, after three or four hours' amusement, I would return to these speculations, they appear so cold, and strained, and ridiculous, that I cannot find in my heart to enter into them any farther.

Hume took an anti-teleological approach to the existence of God, setting himself against the theologians who formed the idea of intelligent design. Instead of the popular ideas of the day, Hume argued that God is a difficult concept that we each put together in our own minds. While he recognized that the degree of detail and equilibrium demonstrated by the physical universe was potentially indicative of having been formed by an intelligent creator, he insisted that there was no solid evidence of God.

He began writing his next book in 1755, but it was not finished and published until 1776. In this text, entitled *Dialogues Concerning Natural Religion*, Hume continues with the subject of the divine. This time, however, instead of focusing on the existence or fallacy of God, Hume attempts to circumvent the issue by switching his subject to that of evil.

Evil was an equally important subject under the umbrella of organized religions of Europe, one that was at the heart of the Catholic and Protestant Churches. There were a series of questions that Hume had to work through in order to determine the role of evil in the world and consider what the answers meant about the existence of God in some form. First, he explained that without God, or a figure of pure good, evil could not exist. Being opposites, one requires the existence of the other. Other questions of importance are, is God unable to combat the evil in the world? Furthermore, if God is against the existence of evil and willing to combat it, then why does evil still exist? Perhaps, God is not actually all-powerful, as the Churches would have its followers believe.

The philosophies described in Hume's masterworks were a clear affront to the variety of religious sects that had sprung up in Europe, the Catholic and Protestant Churches most influential among them. Had Hume published his work a century earlier, there is little doubt that he would have been arrested by the Catholic Inquisition and ultimately put to death for questioning the existence of God and the word of the Bible. In the religious tumult that had taken place between the time of Galileo and Hume, however, rules concerning one's writing and teachings were much less clear. The Catholic Church had less power than it once had, and though Protestant Churches had become less flexible in its own doctrine, the Enlightenment was full of people questioning religious laws; church leaders were beginning to understand that their positions had become less certain.

In Scotland and England, religion was undergoing a series of changes, as were the politics of both countries. Hume, therefore, was unusually safe in the far western reaches of Europe while he contemplated the great problems of the world and society. The society in which he lived, however, was crumbling.

Chapter 21 – Adam Smith

(1723-1790)

Adam Smith, known internationally as the father of modern economics and the leading supporter of laissez-faire financial strategies, was an 18th-century philosopher. Smith grew up in Scotland at a time when the concept of a national economy was concentrated on the gold and silver inventory of each individual country. Imported products from overseas were seen to be harmful because they cost money; export products were considered financially productive because they would bring money back home. For example, nations retained a large network of legal checks to prevent the perceived loss of income through imported goods, such as import charges, exporter grants, and national industrial security.

Smith suggested the concept of an "invisible hand" in his first book, *The Theory of Moral Sentiments*, published in 1759. The term referred to the natural process of free markets to control themselves by means of rivalry, supply and demand, and self-interest. Also recognized for his hypothesis of differential compensation, Smith's idealized model of the free market gave greater salaries to employees in hazardous or undesirable roles. Essentially, Smith believed that if people were free to conduct business as they liked, internationally and domestically, the economy would veer toward wealth as if guided by that invisible hand, without the need of a "real" hand in the form of a monarch or laws. When individuals in such a system reached agreements with each other, Smith theorized that the funds of the nation would be used to achieve the goals that individuals deemed the most important.

In his manuscript, Smith deals widely with charity and natural ethics while simultaneously helping himself to earn the unofficial title of "Father of Capitalism." While much of Smith's economic philosophy is focused on self-interest, *The Theory of Moral Sentiments* is also a treatise on how communication between people depends on empathy. Humans sympathize with others naturally, he wrote, and this helps them to know how their conduct can be moderated to preserve the social balance. The empathy at the foundation of our personal thoughts and experiences, Smith believed, guides our behavior. He wrote, "How selfish soever man may be supposed, there are evidently some principles in his nature, which interest him in the fortune of others, and render their happiness necessary to him, though he derives nothing from it except the pleasure of seeing it."[35]

A member of the British intelligentsia, Adam Smith was firm friends with other important figures of the Enlightenment and Industrial Revolution, including James Watt—the inventor of the steam engine—and philosopher David Hume. An active member of the ongoing Republic of Letters, Smith relocated to France in 1763 to become a personal tutor to the stepson of Charles Townshend, the future Chancellor of the Exchequer. During his stay in France, Smith penned his most popular book, *An Inquiry into the Nature and Causes of the Wealth of Nations*.

---

[35] Smith, Adam. *The Theory of Moral Sentiments.* 1759. [19] Rae, John. *Life of Adam Smith.* 1895.

The book explained a practical use for the revised financial hypotheses in order to substitute free market systems for mercantile and physiocratic ones, the latter having become outdated during the industrial advancement of the era. The 18th century was, for Europe in particular, less a world sustained solely on exports and agriculture and more a world in which commerce and manufacturing played a large role.

There were five sections contained in the pages of the *Wealth of Nations*, in which Smith separately addressed the broad topics of labor, stocks, long-term wealth, the political-economic system, and taxation under a monarch or sovereign leader. Detailed and ambitious about the potential of Europe's future, Smith's book surprised its publishers by selling out in six months. The *Wealth of Nations* was widely read—or at least claimed to have been read—by members of the British Parliament, even inspiring Prime Minister Lord Frederick North to register a sale of property tax and man-servant tax as described in the book.

Other politicians, such as Charles James Fox, mentioned the book during public events but admitted to friends later on that they had not understood the content of *Wealth of Nations* and therefore had not actually read it.[19] Nevertheless, Smith was summoned to meetings with Scottish and English political representatives to discuss theories of taxation and potential trade agreements, such as those with Ireland, for example.

Ultimately, Adam Smith's books helped launch an immense paradigm shift within Europe—and then in America—from medieval economic systems into the laissez-faire model. Laissez-faire is a financial regime in which private business operations are kept separate from the rules and regulations of the government. Laissez-faire advocates claim that the king, sovereign, or state government should be kept completely out of the economy. The idea that the government or the monarch should be kept out of decision-making was not new; it had earlier been suggested by Vincent de

Gournay, a physiocrat economist who believed that agriculture should be unlegislated.

Philosophically, Smith's vision of laissez-faire economics went hand in hand with the ideas of individual freedom that characterized the Enlightenment. While people sought equal access to education, jobs, and opportunities without the traditional entanglement of social pedigrees and royal charters, businessmen wanted the same freedom to set up companies and make as much money as possible. The possibilities seemed endless to Europe's newly emerged liberal class, if only they could get out from under the yoke of regime and regulations. As far as Adam Smith was concerned, having all sorts of individual freedom, including those that would affect businessmen, would result in benefits for the entire world.

As Scotland, Britain, and their neighbors moved into the 19th century, Adam Smith's economic teachings fundamentally changed not only how business was conducted but also how nations counted their compiled wealth. During the Middle Ages, European countries would compare their wealth according to their own reserves of gold, silver, and precious gems. According to Smith's assessment, however, this changed into a measure of national wealth that was directly related to manufacturing and trade. The shift culminated in the establishment of the Gross Domestic Product, or GDP: a metric by which the market value of all goods and services produced within a country is represented.

Adam Smith's books and political relationships urged Europe into the modern capitalist era, based on the belief that independent businesses would provide not only for themselves but also for the rest of the population.

Chapter 22– The Boston Tea Party

(1773)

Despite the fact that the British Empire was immense in size and resources, Britain was heavily in debt in the 1760s. Desperate for some way to refill their coffers, the British Parliament came up with a new taxation plan that was expected to cover the outlandish costs of continual war, colonialism, and an outdated economic model. One of the main tenets of the plan was a tax hike on imported tea in the American colonies.

The British government and King George III felt these charges were perfectly fair, given that a large percentage of its kingdom's debt was caused from helping the American colonists help subdue the native tribes during the French and Indian War, a war which was fought as part of the Seven Years' War, meaning it was fought more for the benefit of the British than the colonists. The colonists, on the other hand, felt quite differently, particularly because they were already forbidden from purchasing tea from anyone other than the British East India Company. They also believed that, as British subjects, they were entitled to receive the full support of the British Parliament and the British Army without having to suffer under ever-increasing taxation.

The new taxes included the 1765 Stamp Act and the Townshend Acts, which increased the prices American colonists had to pay for items like journals, paper, building materials, mirrors, fruit, and tea. Though several of these taxes were later dropped following harsh criticisms and protests from the colonists, the lucrative tax on tea remained. The colonists bought millions of British pounds' worth of tea each year, so while this tax cost the settlers a great deal, it was incredibly profitable for Britain. The monarchy was not willing to let go of such a lucrative deal when it was needed the most, and thus, the first protest leading up to the American War of Independence was set in motion.

On December 16th, 1773, a band of settlers at Griffin's Wharf, Massachusetts, decided they had paid quite enough to the British Crown. It was a breaking point for many people in the British American colonies, and they were furious at the imposition of taxation without Britain allowing American officials to serve in the British Parliament. Determined not to spend another coin on Crown taxes, protesters pushed 342 containers of tea, weighing an approximate total of 9,000 kilograms (about 2,000 pounds), from the British East India Company into the harbor.[36] The protest was led by a group of revolutionaries who identified themselves as the Sons of Liberty. The group included Benedict Arnold and Paul Revere, who had been orchestrating meetings where they and other members of the group decried British rule.

The colonists had already been boycotting tea sent to their harbors by the British, instead opting to smuggle in affordable Dutch tea to stock their cupboards. Losing millions of pounds of income and now having had quantities of such a precious commodity wasted away in the Atlantic Ocean during what was quickly dubbed the Boston Tea Party, the British Parliament decided to pass the Intolerable Acts in 1774.

---

[36] "Boston Tea Party." *History.* Web. 2019.

The Intolerable Acts consisted of a variety of laws designed to removed Massachusetts' self-governance and freedoms, causing further riots and opposition in the thirteen colonies. The British Parliament expected that these punitive policies would counter the tendency toward colonial protest, but it had quite the opposite effect. The Quebec Act, added separately to the new legislation inflicted upon the colonies, changed the border of the British colony of Quebec to include Ohio and other modern Midwest states. It was just further punishment to the American colonies to have some of their lands given to the Canadian colonies.

Defiant in the wake of their rebellion and punishments, the Sons of Liberty formed a splinter group known as the Patriots, and they came together to organize their own governing body. A conference of delegates from twelve of the thirteen British colonies that would one day become the United States of America established the First Continental Congress. It met in Philadelphia, Pennsylvania, from September 5th to October 26th in 1774. The participants were elected by the people of their region or by local committees. Though not all the attendees were of the same mind regarding how to deal with the situation, eventually, they agreed on a course of action. The congressmen agreed to support the boycott of British products and not a demand for outright independence. After all, there was still a high level of loyalty to the British Crown during those years in the American colonies. All they needed, however, was a push in the right direction to start calling for a republic. And the right people for the job were already hard at work.

Chapter 23 – Thomas Paine

(1737-1809)

Thomas Paine, born in England in 1737, emigrated to America and became a political activist, philosopher, and revolutionary. Having corresponded frequently with Benjamin Franklin through the Republic of Letters, Paine decided to become an American and participate in the upcoming War of Independence. He arrived on the other side of the Atlantic Ocean just one year prior to the outbreak of war at the age of 37.

Once positioned in the British American colonies, Paine wrote a pamphlet by the name *Common Sense*, which quickly became the most popular piece of literature in the colonies. In an attempt to lay the basis for a republican government in the colonies, Paine referred heavily to several Enlightenment concepts such as the "natural state," written about by John Locke. Though humankind's natural state was to band together in small, peaceful groups, Paine said that the more people come together, the more likely evil is to present itself in society—since, according to Paine, evil was inherent in humanity and would always be there under the surface. To prevent such evil, therefore, *Common Sense* advocated for a sensible government to rein it in.

As for the monarchal system imposed upon the British American colonies from afar, Paine argued that such monarchies strip away humanity's natural rights to freedom and equality. The social differences between kings and their subjects, Paine believed, was entirely based on false beliefs about the sanctity of royal families. This premise is where Paine differed from Locke, who believed in a constitutional monarchy. Paine advocated a system of government in which there was no monarch whatsoever since the tendency of any king or queen is to recover their power, whatever the law may say.

Given the contemporary state of relations between the colonists and the British, Paine wrote that the best course of action was to declare independence and create a brand-new type of government by the people. His vision culminated in the establishment of the Continental Conference, which would house seven elected representatives from each of the existing British American colonies, with the same method potentially being used to elect members of a governing Congress.

When he first arrived in the colonies, Paine discovered that many people still held the British Crown—then held by King George III—in high esteem, but his writing and networking managed to sway a great deal of them toward the promise of independence. The timing of the publication of *Common Sense* was ideal for the debate amongst the colonists about whether to seek independence for themselves, given that the king's Proclamation of Rebellion arrived in America at the same time.

The pamphlet was very effective because of Paine's wonderful marketing strategy. With the first version, which was released around the same time as King George III's announcement on the colonists' ideas, he sought to oppose the powerful monarchical gesture with the highly anti-monarchical *Common Sense*.

In his book, *The Age of Reason; Being an Investigation of True and Fabulous Theology*, first published in 1794 with the last part published in 1807, Thomas Paine wrote the following passages, in which he worried how religious fanaticism might have a negative impact on the colonists' future.

> People in general know not what wickedness there is in this pretended word of God. Brought up in habits of superstition, they take it for granted that the Bible is true, and that it is good; they permit themselves not to doubt of it, and they carry the ideas they form of the benevolence of the Almighty to the book which they have been taught to believe was written by his authority. Good heavens! it is quite another thing, it is a book of lies, wickedness, and blasphemy...

> Be this as it may, they decided by vote which of the books out of the collection they had made, should be the WORD OF GOD, and which should not. They rejected several; they voted others to be doubtful, such as the books called the Apocrypha; and those books which had a majority of votes, were voted to be the word of God. Had they voted otherwise, all the people since calling themselves Christians had believed otherwise; for the belief of the one comes from the vote of the other.

Paine considered himself foremost an American citizen, but his British birth landed him in trouble several times while visiting France. Nevertheless, he persevered in search of financial support for the American War of Independence and returned to America in August of 1781 with a large amount of gold. Though details are sparse in the documentation of this journey, historians generally believe that Paine traveled to France thanks to an idea from Benjamin Franklin. He most likely met with the French king face to face, but it is known that Paine's cargo was very much appreciated back in the United States.

On a later journey to France during the Terror of Paris, Paine was arrested once more. He blamed American General George Washington for conspiring to have him put in prison, and Paine wrote a scathing treatise on the subject. Upon being released, he traveled between England, France, and America several times, eventually returning to the latter in the early years of the 19th century. Though Thomas Paine had had a large hand in sculpting and shaping the American Revolution, he had lost all popularity due to his ongoing political arguments with men like George Washington.

When he died in 1809 in New York City, only six people came to Thomas Paine's funeral.[37]

[37] "Thomas Paine." USHistory.org. Web.

Chapter 24 – The American Revolution

(1776-1783)

Thanks to the Republic of Letters and frequent travel across the Atlantic Ocean, the Enlightenment was happening in Europe and the Americas at much the same time, and it hit a high point in the 18th century. In the United States, intellectuals such as Thomas Paine, Thomas Jefferson, and Benjamin Franklin took the ideas of their European counterparts to heart, having a huge impact on the future of their own country. The American Revolution of the late 18th century happened shortly before the French Revolution, both of which involved the modernization of science, logic, politics, and religion.

The American Enlightenment further supported the concept of the country as a republic, which was revolutionary in and of itself at a time when monarchs ruled the nations of Europe. The thinkers of the American Enlightenment imagined a system in which the head of state would be popularly chosen, not designated on the merits of inheritance. The colonists and American-born residents of the colonies believed more as time went on that theirs should be a nation independent of Great Britain; many also considered the latter to be an evil empire. To separate themselves from their perceived oppressors, the various communities of the United States gathered armies, eventually amassing some of them under the banner of the American Continental Army. This army was led by General George Washington.

The Continental Army was officially united in 1775, and Washington, after being elected its leader by his peers, showed his commitment to the cause by refusing to collect a salary. Soon afterward, Washington was bound for Boston in response to American riots. The Boston Tea Party had taken place there less than two years earlier, and the same location was to be the site where the American Revolutionary War finally broke out.

In the winter of 1775, Congress ordered the army to carry out an invasion of the northern regions of British North America that same summer, but Washington disagreed with the plan. Nevertheless, Patriot and Son of Liberty member Benedict Arnold led the attack. Having entered the Continental Army immediately upon its creation, Arnold had already participated in a joint military operation in which the American revolutionaries seized the British garrison at Fort Ticonderoga in New York. It was the first victory of the Revolutionary War.

Quebec, held by British defenders, staved off the American invaders and reduced the numbers of the attacking soldiers by half. The plan was quickly abandoned in favor of fortifying the regions to the south, and the Canadians—still a century away from being united under their own confederation agreement—chose sides as they saw fit. Ultimately, however, Quebec and the rest of the northern colonies remained loyal to the British Crown.

During the American Revolution, Thomas Jefferson served as the governor of Virginia. He would one day be the president of the United States from 1801 to 1809, but before he took on that prestigious role, Jefferson was integral to the beliefs and success of the American revolutionaries. Although considered a major spokesperson for democracy and republicanism in the age of the Enlightenment, some contemporaries and historians criticized Jefferson's personal situation, which included many slaves working in his fields.

Jefferson was the principal author of the Declaration of Independence, which was written as the fundamental political document of the newborn United States of America. Although Congress edited the final version of the document, Thomas Jefferson came up with a great deal of the social and political content contained in it. In June 1776, a little over a year after the war started, Jefferson chose his words for the Declaration of Independence, capitalizing on the long-held belief of the colonists in their independence from Great Britain. He was influenced by Locke's and Montesquieu's illuminating theses, as well as by John Adams, an influential member of Congress.

Enlightenment ideals were at the root of many of the American Revolution's concepts. The rebels in search of sovereignty formed a group whose aims centered on the liberty of expression, equality, freedom of the press, and tolerance of religion. When Jefferson revealed his work on the Declaration of Independence to his fellow rebels, the words became almost instantly famous:

> We hold these Truths to be self-evident: that all Men are created equal; that they are endowed by their creator with inherent and certain inalienable Rights; that among these are life, liberty, & the pursuit of happiness. That to secure these rights, Governments are instituted among Men, deriving their just powers from the consent of the governed, That whenever any Form of Government becomes destructive of these ends, it is the Right of the People to alter or to abolish it, and to institute new Government, laying its foundation on such principles, and organizing its powers in such form, as to

them shall seem most likely to effect their Safety and Happiness.[38]

Chapter 25 – François-Marie Arouet (Voltaire)

(1789-1799)

Because of a declining economy that kept them starving, freezing, and unable to care for themselves and their relatives, the French people were unwilling to take any more abuses as the 18th century came to a close. King Louis XV had spent the country into heavy debt, which he then passed onto his grandson, King Louis XVI, and the latter could not adopt the needed modifications to the tax legislation in order to deal with the matter. What the people had begun to realize was that they had the capacity to engage in choices regarding the state and to enjoy personal liberties, which took the form of the philosophies of the Enlightenment.

One of the most vital of these philosophers was François-Marie Arouet, better known as Voltaire. Voltaire was born in 1694 and published works in almost every literary form, including poems, essays, and novels, and he wrote on the topics of science, government, and civil liberties until he died in 1778. As a Frenchman in support of governance by the people, his views were very controversial at the time, so much so that he was banished to England in 1726 for his ideas. Under King George I of England, followed shortly after by King George II, and Prime Minister Robert Walpole, he researched constitutional monarchy and felt that his country lacked political philosophy.

Voltaire wrote:

> I have wanted to kill myself a hundred times, but somehow I am still in love with life. This ridiculous weakness is perhaps one of our more stupid melancholy propensities, for is there anything more stupid than to be eager to go on carrying a burden which one would gladly throw away, to loathe one's very being and yet to hold it fast, to fondle the snake that devours us until it has eaten our hearts away?[39]

Voltaire thought that the future of France rested in the removal of priests and the privileges of the nobility. He saw England's constitutional monarchy and how it operated firsthand, and he was motivated by the way it permitted its people a freer spiritual and civil existence. While the aristocratic classes in France were untaxed, the nobility of England added to their nation's coffers so that the common people, in particular, were given greater care. Voltaire described the many ways he thought France could be enhanced by pursuing the example of England in a collection called *Letters on the English*, which was published for the French public.

The series of essays represented England in a flattering light and were, therefore, considered to be highly offensive to the French monarchy. Voltaire's work describes the Quakers, Presbyterians, Church of England, Arians, Parliament, government, commerce, health, science, mathematics, and a number of well-known individuals in England.

In comparing the staunch French Catholicism of his own country with the liberal attitude of the Quakers, Voltaire discovered he favored the latter. Quakers frequently gathered together for

---

[39] 22 Voltaire.
Candide.
1759.

intellectual discussion and were not baptized or required to take communion. The French writer also appreciated the Anglican religion, which was developed by England's King Henry VIII in the 16th century, although he was dissatisfied with the fact that there were still so many facets of Catholicism present in the religion.

Voltaire's philosophies were primarily focused on religion, but it was his parliamentary and fiscal ideas that had the most influence upon France's middle class. In England, the legislature was an extensive group of males whose aim was to debate problems of the day and reach an accord with the ruling king. Taxes, which had been developed constantly for hundreds of years, were intended to be used for the good of the country. In addition, the constitutional monarchy was designed to reasonably accumulate and distribute such revenues, not simply hand them over to the monarch and the aristocracy.

The thoughts of the English philosopher John Locke were perhaps most important of all to Voltaire. Some call Locke "the father of liberalism," but others call him the man who created European empiricism. He was a logical thinker who trusted in developing theories based on empirical or strong information— from state affairs to faith to science. This was an uncommon concept for individuals who had been ruled by the power of the French kings and the clergy since they were born. It was even a little crazy and revolutionary that individuals could have the capacity and freedom to believe their own versions of truth and read the source materials for themselves.

Voltaire was interested not only in philosophy but also in hard science. He read Newton's books concerning natural laws and started to imagine what sort of natural laws there may be governing the social order of mankind. Voltaire was not alone in his studies, either; he studied and philosophized with the assistance of Émilie du Châtelet, his long-standing romantic partner.

Émilie du Châtelet was a woman whose intellect was able to flourish during the Enlightenment thanks to her aristocratic background. Noted for her charm and wit, du Châtelet worked her way into the scientific circles of Paris, becoming the well-known lover of Voltaire. Like Voltaire, Châtelet was a natural philosopher but also an eager mathematician. At the age of nineteen, she was married to the Marquis Florent-Claude du Chastelet-Lomont, and she had the money and the freedom to hire a series of tutors to help her learn the complexities of the higher forms of mathematics. She was still married throughout her relationship with Voltaire, though this was not uncommon in 17th-century France.

Du Châtelet was often turned out of Paris' famous salons and cafés when she tried to join the men's intellectual discussions within, but she did not let such sexist and unfair treatment dissuade her from her goals. On at least one occasion, she simply found a set of men's clothes and disguised herself before joining a café circle. These events inspired her to study even harder to earn the same education as had her contemporary male friends and family.

Eager to put her expert mathematics and natural philosophical skills to good use, Châtelet set herself upon the grand task of translating Isaac Newton's *Principia* into French, her own native language. Du Châtelet often wrote about the physical sciences, while Voltaire preferred to criticize social classes and religions. They both contributed to many important discussions and works that not only spread the knowledge of science throughout France but also bolstered the growing belief that France should empower its own citizens to have more control over their lives and their country.

Before the French Revolution, Voltaire, du Châtelet, Locke, Newton, Montesquieu, and many of their fellow Enlightenment counterparts had already died, but the broad acceptance of the ideas they had about reform, poverty, and religion had been fundamental to the central movement of the Enlightenment. These philosophies of individual rights and a government comprised of diverse people were central to turning the tide in France. Several other philosophers were working in France and elsewhere in Europe, echoing Voltaire's feelings. His theories helped reform France, Europe, and the New World irrevocably, cultivating a massive rebellion that saw the overthrow of the French monarchy and the installation of the realm's first   republic.

Chapter 26 – Mary Somerville

(1780-1872)

Mary Somerville was the second child of four surviving children in a genteel but poor family in Scotland. Her father worked in the Royal Navy, but his pay remained low despite several rank increases. Mary's mother did what she could to add to the household's wages by selling vegetables and cow's milk. These same chores were taught to Mary and her siblings early on. There was little time for education, and as far as Mary's parents were concerned, their daughter did not need to worry about more than reading, writing, basic sums, and household duties. Mary learned to read from her mother, who taught from the Bible and other Calvinist publications.

Reading was Mary's favorite pastime, apart from playing outside with the birds, and she later commented in her memoir that she would take the opportunity to read from the family's well-stocked library during bad weather. After all, few outside chores could be attempted during a storm. Unfortunately, she was soon turned out of the library to attend sewing classes in the village, as it was expected of her to create an embroidery sampler. This interruption of her reading sessions fostered a dislike of the traditional role of women early on in life. She wondered why a girl would be given the natural curiosity to learn if she was not going to be allowed to pursue the knowledge which interested her the most.

Mary's first husband, her distant cousin Lieutenant Samuel Greig (not to be confused with Admiral Samuel Greig, his father), did not believe there was any reason for a woman to pursue academic studies. She was allowed to study, but her primary job was caring for their two children. Greig died in 1807, after which point Mary and the children went back home to their family house in Scotland.[40] She studied there and made the acquaintance of the man who would become her second husband: William Somerville.

William Somerville was an army physician who supported and respected his wife's intellect. When William was appointed to the Royal Society of London, both he and Mary benefited from a closer look at the world of science. Both Mary and William were enraptured by the leading sciences of the day. Their friends included astronomers, philosophers, and scientists, and they often met with leading European mathematicians and physicists who visited London. The couple traveled often and cultivated a personal social circle of highly-esteemed scientists in London, Paris, and beyond. All of these people met regularly, and many corresponded though the Republic of Letters.

Thanks to her network, Mary Somerville was invited to translate Pierre-Simon Laplace's book, *Mécanique Céleste*, into English. Laplace was a French engineer and mathematician whose book transformed classical engineering from a geometric-focused study to one based on calculus. Once the translation was completed by Somerville in 1831, the work was retitled *The Mechanism of the Heavens*. It was an instantaneous success in terms of copies sold and critical acclaim. Somerville happily tackled numerous other translations within the scientific community, which greatly improved

---

[40] Martha Somerville. *Personal Recollections, from Early Life to Old Age, of Mary Somerville: With Selections from Her Correspondence.* 1874.

the flow of information between the various countries of Europe. Her reputation among scientists at home and abroad was very positive, though nothing made her stand out among them as peers quite like designing and running her own scientific experiment.

Mary was not just inspired by scientists—she was one in her own right. While her husband practiced medicine and kept up to date on the discoveries of contemporary doctoring, Mary performed experiments and documented them carefully. In fact, she revealed her first scientific paper, *The Magnetic Properties of the Violet Rays of the Solar Spectrum*, to the Royal Academy in 1826.[41] Ultraviolet light was a very popular topic in 19th-century England, and it was discussed regularly within the Royal Society. Mary designed her own experiments to test the highly-touted hypothesis that ultraviolet light could impart a magnetic field onto other objects.

Mary Somerville was one of the first women admitted into the Royal Society of London due to her merits as a scientist, though ironically, she was not allowed to read her research paper to the all-male group. She visited the prestigious club in 1834 with William so that her research could be presented to the club, with her husband reading the essay in her stead. As demeaning as this was, it was Somerville's research that led the English philosopher William Whewell to coin the term "scientist" in his 1834 review of one of Mary's papers.[42] After all, she couldn't be addressed as the usual "man of science," so, therefore, a new term was necessary.

The experiment Mary's husband described to the Royal Society was designed to test the theorized magnetic properties of ultraviolet light. First, through a glass prism, she focused a ray of light in order to separate white light into its seven components: red, orange, yellow, green, blue, indigo, and violet. Next, she concentrated the violet

---

[41] Lindemann, Kate. "Mary Fairfax Grieg Somerville." *Society for the Study of Women Philosophers*. Web.

[42] Whewell, William. "On the Connexion of the Physical Sciences. By Mrs. Somerville". *Quarterly Review* vol. LI, no. CI, March 1834.

light onto a steel needle to impart any intrinsic magnetic characteristics into the metal. The needle was placed in a pan to see if it was pointing to the polar north to check its magnetism. Her tests showed that after exposure to violet light, the experimental pins took on magnetic properties.

Writing was a passion of Somerville's, and she had a talent for taking complicated scientific topics and summing them up in a way every reader could understand. Her 1848 book *Physical Geography* was not only the first geography textbook in English, but it also remained the primary text for students until the early 20th century. The text explains both the landmass and water structures of the Earth but also the apparent structure of the solar system. Everything from the physical characteristics of lakes and rivers to the Earth's position relative to its planetary neighbors was included. Somerville received the Victoria Gold Medal from the Royal Geographer's Society for her contribution to the field.

Epilogue

The major takeaways from the Enlightenment period in Europe and North America are the search for a rigid, modernized scientific method, peace between religious groups, and the separation of church and state affairs. It also clearly involved a host of women who were crying out to be taken seriously as human beings capable of much more than what they were allowed to pursue.

The urgent call for a regimented and controlled approach to science during the Enlightenment had a big impact on modern science. Internationally, scientists of today subscribe to the scientific method, in which they collect measurable evidence through experimentation. The evidence is contrasted and compared to the scientist's prior hypothesis, and the results are either used to support or negate their theory.

The same method is taught to young students in school when they are tasked with putting together a science experiment or science project. First, children come up with a question to test, such as, "What happens when a volcano explodes?" Then, they write down their own hypothesis as to what the answer might be. Through research and experimentation, they learn how their expectations differed or were similar to reality.

In religious terms, the Enlightenment saw the birth of many diverse religious sects, mostly based in Christianity but all struggling for autonomy. As a result of contemporary philosophizing and many viewpoints on theology, people were able to explore what their own minds told them about the truth of God and religion. As more and more people sought personal truth in their relationship with the Church, more types of Christianity appeared. These were forced to forge alliances with one another, firstly against the Catholic Church and eventually against one another until all were allowed to remain without judgment.

As for the women of the age, their words are just as emotive now as they ever were. It was thanks to the hard work and dedication of females like Mary Somerville, Bathsua Makin, and Marie du Moulin that women today are educated alongside men and able to pursue careers in many different fields. The long road toward equality—between the sexes and belief systems—still stretches onward.

Check out more books by Captivating History

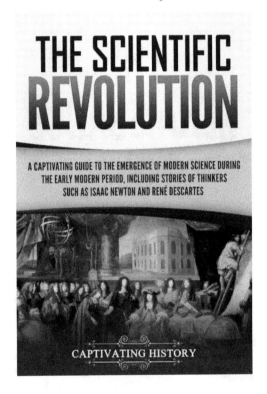

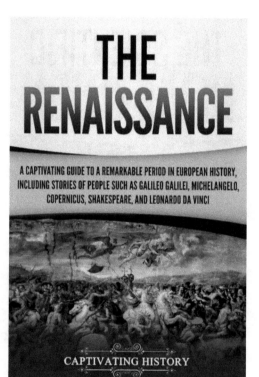

CPSIA information can be obtained
at www.ICGtesting.com
Printed in the USA
LVHW080849250920
667082LV00018B/266